THE
MEETING

Tim Fulton

ISBN 978-0-578-77567-8

Copyright 2020

Dedication
Jansen Chazanof

I dedicate this book to Jansen Chazanof - a good friend, trusted mentor, and the best Vistage Chair I ever met. He died Monday, March 12, 2018 in a tragic car accident.

Jansen was a Vistage Chair for 15 years, and prior to that he was an executive in numerous organizations. As a Chair, he was the recipient of many awards including Chair of Excellence. After his retirement, he was named Vistage Chair Emeritus.

Jansen loved keeping bees, riding his recumbent bike, spending time with family, and helping people in any way he possibly could. I remember him for his infectious smile, piercing interrogatories, and a heart of gold.

Thank you Jansen...

Small Business Matters
The Meeting.

Once upon a time, there was a peer group of small business CEOs that met to help increase the effectiveness and enhance the lives of its members.

Every month, the group meets for a full day to share their issues, learn from speakers, and enjoy the company of other like-minded executives.

One month, the group met and tackled four very common and yet important small business issues.

Because of that meeting, the members learned much more about those specific business issues than they would have known otherwise.

Because of that meeting, four members were able to successfully address their specific business issues and continue to grow their businesses.

Until finally; the meeting ended, the members returned to their businesses and their lives and looked forward to next month's group meeting.

Table of Contents

CHAPTER 1
PROLOGUE

"Each meeting occurs at the precise moment for which it was meant. Usually, when it will have the greatest impact on our lives."
– Nadia Scrieva, Fathoms of Forgiveness

It's 4:50 a.m.

Only Moe the dog looks forward more to getting up this early on a weekday than his owner. He knows there is a walk in his immediate future and he's poised and ready to dart out the front door.

But this is not just any day. This is meeting day. It's Vistage day and Vistage Chair Bud Irvine vaults out of bed two minutes before his alarm is scheduled to ring. Bud usually wakes up before his alarm goes off and this day is no exception. This is a big day. It's meeting day.

Twenty minutes later and about 10 miles intown, Vistage member Danny Goodall was a little slower to rise out of bed. He attended a dinner event with several of his old fraternity brothers from UGA and he is regretting that last glass of Cabernet. Danny was hosting his Vistage group at his office and he had work to do before to the members showing up at 8 a.m.

Danny Goodall has hosted the Vistage group before and he was confident that his Powerpoint presentation was almost ready to share with the members. He has a few last-minute updates to the one-page business plan he will run through with the group. He also needs to take one final look at his financial dashboard. He knows several of the members will want to question his decision to add a new COO.

"What have I forgotten?" wondered Danny as he got dressed and prepared to go to the kitchen for what will be his first of several cups of highly caffeinated coffee.

At this same moment and 30 miles north of Atlanta in Forsyth County, Vistage member Tex Alexander was slow to get out of bed. Tex had played football at Georgia Tech 10 years earlier and endures the aches and pains that go with playing four years at that level. Two bad knees, a hip injury, and a bad back collectively make getting out of bed in the morning a painful experience.

Almost as painful, was the thought of discussing his "terrorist" with the Vistage group that day. Tex had his one-to-one meeting with group Chair Bud Irvine the week prior and had promised to be prepared to bring this issue to the group meeting today. He acknowledged to Bud that he should have fired the executive months ago and had not. He is fearful of the repercussions of such a decision on the rest of his business.

"What will the group think of me now?" he wondered as he had procrastinated on this decision for months.

It was now 6:30 a.m. and Vistage member Ray Jernath was still in bed. He, too, was planning to attend the meeting that day. He, too, had promised

Bud to finally share his exit strategy from the business with the group. His was a third-generation family business that he had been with for the past thirty two years. "Why do I need to have an exit plan?" he thought while still in bed. "Exit where?" he wondered out loud.

Phil Balmer had been up for hours. His business partner had been missing for several weeks and now he had to go to explain what he was prepared to do. This was not the first time he had brought this issue to his group. But this time was it felt different. This time he was ready to take action.

"It's time for a divorce!" Phil said to himself as he loaded his Chevy Suburban with his work backpack and a change of clothes for his son's football practice after work.

Vistage is a 60-year old international CEO membership organization, the first and largest of its kind. Bud Irvine, 58, has been a Vistage Chair for 15 years. As a Chair, he is responsible for organizing and facilitating a monthly meeting for 16 small business CEOs. The businesses range in size from a $4 million technology business to a $60 million residential development company.

Bud is responsible for three Vistage groups, and this one is his toughest. Each of the CEO members shows up for that monthly meeting thinking they should probably be somewhere else on that particular day. They are very busy executives leading fast-paced lives. And yet they know that this day is unlike any other that month. For this one day a month, they are not in charge. They attend this meeting to learn, to find answers to their questions and to question their own answers.

They also attend this peer-group meeting to help each other by asking tough questions, by probing and investigating each other's businesses and their lives. A code of confidentiality ensures that members bring their toughest issues and decisions to the group and that everything discussed in the meeting stays within the group. It's the Las Vegas rule at its best.

It's meeting day.

CHAPTER TWO
THE WALK

*"All truly great thoughts are
conceived while walking"*
– Friedrich Nietzsche

The science of happiness suggests that there are five key ingredients to forging a happier life. They are meditation, regular exercise, journaling, being grateful, and random acts of kindness (RAKs). Bud figures he is able to knock out at least two of the five every morning during his walk with Moe.

A thirty-minute walk in a quiet suburban Atlanta neighborhood at 530 a.m. is as close to a meditative state as Bud has ever been. His mind wanders from the highlights of the past day to what lies ahead for the next 12 hours. It's the fastest 30 minutes of the day as his mind slips in and out of a deep thinking state of consciousness.

Moe on the other hand is hard at work. Off leash he is running from yard to yard investigating every interesting scent he encounters. Occasionally he will track down a squirrel or a possum which will distract him enough to lose sight of his master. Fortunately, his keen sense of smell will bring him back to Bud, only to go chasing another target soon after.

On several occasions, Bud has arrived back home without Moe only to have the Golden Lab show up a few minutes later sprinting along the home street determined not to miss his morning feeding.

On this particular walk, Bud is giving much thought to his Vistage meeting that day. Like the director of a theatre production, he is considering the agenda (the script) for the day, the members (the actors), and the potential outcomes (the reviews) of the meeting.

While he has facilitated hundreds of these group meetings before, Bud realizes that each one is unique. Each meeting tells a different story. Each meeting produces different results for the members. Each meeting provides a unique set of circumstances for the Chair to arrange and direct.

There is always a healthy dose of stress for Bud with each meeting. Is he ready for the meeting? Who will show up, or more importantly, who will not show for the meeting? What issues will arise from the members? The more uncertainty the greater the stress for this experienced Chair.

It's now 6 a.m. and Bud and his accomplice Moe have arrived back home. Moe is indulging in his first feeding of the day and Bud focuses on preparations for today's meeting.

CHAPTER THREE
THE CHAIR

"Two roads diverged in the wood, and I -
I took the one less traveled by, and that
has made all the difference."
– Robert Frost

Bud Irvine didn't grow up in Miami, Fl., wanting to be a Vistage Chair. Bud initially wanted to be a professional athlete. He was very competitive and played as many youth sports as he could find.

Despite his ambitions and no shortage of desire, Bud was never much better than average as a young athlete. There were not going to be any college coaches clamoring over Bud to play at their prestigious universities.

Next, Bud set his sights on being an attorney. He envisioned an Ivy League education, maybe Princeton, leading to becoming a top litigator. This may have been a product of watching shows like "Ironside" with Raymond Burr, "Matlock" with Andy Griffith, and "The Paper Chase" and Professor Kingsfield.

However, although Bud was a good student in secondary school, he was not good enough for Princeton, and the thought of becoming a famous lawyer slowly evaporated by his senior year in high school. It seemed like a lot more schooling and intellectual effort than he was prepared to commit to.

In his senior year, Bud turned his attention to coaching. He began to coach Little League basketball and baseball. He found he really enjoyed working with younger kids and helping them improve their skills. He also found he enjoyed developing his own skills as a coach and a strategist.

Bud had an entrepreneurial spirit as a child. First, he first delivered newspapers on his bicycle. Next, he started a lawn-cutting business for his neighborhood. He also bought and sold collectibles like bumper stickers in school.

Early on, Bud had a keen interest in different ways of making money. He gained key insights into cash flow (never run out), inventory management (never run out), and customer service (under-promise, over-deliver).

In his senior year of high school, Bud earned early admission to the University of Florida. He was looking forward to becoming a Florida Gator. Then he made a Spring break trip to New Orleans with his dad to visit Tulane University, where he fell in love with the city and the school. Goodbye Gainesville, hello New Orleans.

Bud spent five years at Tulane studying economics, meeting interesting people from around the world, and spending perhaps too much time in the

French Quarter. He initially wanted to pursue a teaching/coaching major but was told by his father that the tuition for a private and prestigious institution like Tulane didn't align well with a job as a teacher. Hence, a major in Economics followed by an MBA that followed equipped Bud with the education he needed to move into a professional career.

In his final year in college, Bud interviewed with several businesses; a beer distributorship, a large hotel chain, and a bank. The thought of working for any of these companies, aside from the free beer, did little to capture his professional imagination. Bud had an entrepreneurial gene and wanted to pursue his own business venture.

At the time of Bud's college graduation in 1981, his father worked as a general manager of a large retail tire distribution business in South Florida. One store he had a financial interest in was underperforming and at risk of going out of business.

The night of Bud's graduation in New Orleans, he and his dad decided over drinks that Bud would be a good fit to take over management of that failing business and attempt a turnaround. It was at this time that the young entrepreneur would learn two important lessons in business. First, do your homework before making a big career decision. This turnaround effort was going to turn out to be much tougher than he anticipated. Second, never make significant decisions late at night in a bar past your third drink.

The tire store in South Miami had been run by a friend of Bud's dad who was a fifty percent owner. It was a family business. The manager was a retired Air Force captain. He was accompanied in the business by his wife and two sons. For several years the business did very well with consistent growth and above average profits. Then, the captain went AWOL and his family members labored to keep the business afloat.

Bud unknowingly walked into a three-ring circus his first day at Banner Tire. The store manager had been AWOL for six months. His wife, with little business acumen, was running the show. The two sons came and went as they desired, as did the store's inventory, tools, and cash. The other employees were both spectators and accomplices to the festivities that took place each day in the store.

Over the next five years, Bud was able to clean up the business, remove the family members, build a new store, and then sell the business for a fair price to a friendly competitor. Lots of lessons learned for the novice business leader.

For the next ten years, Bud continued to exercise his entrepreneurial muscles opening, growing, and then exiting a variety of different small businesses. Some were more successful than others. There were lessons learned with each venture.

As Bud earned his stripes as a business owner, he also found that he enjoyed being around other business owners. Talking shop. Trading stories. Sharing best practices. These efforts combined with reading every business book he could get his hands on accelerated his growth in small business and also expanded his desire to help others.

In 1994, Bud Irvine started his own small business consulting practice, **Small Business Matters.** He began coaching other small business operators, offering training programs , and facilitating off-site executive strategic meetings. This was a great opportunity to leverage his own 12 years of entrepreneurial experience, both good and bad, as a small business owner.

Bud's Vistage career started in 2003. At that time the name of the company was TEC which stood for The Executive Committee. One of Bud's best friends was a TEC member who encouraged Bud to explore becoming a TEC Chair, the leader responsible for facilitating the monthly group meetings.

Bud looked into this new career opportunity and found it was exactly what he was looking for - an opportunity to work with growth-minded small business CEO's in small groups while feeding his own growth needs at the same time. TEC's mission statement read "Increasing the Effectiveness and Enhancing the Lives of CEO's. This was perfect.

TEC was started in 1957 by a CEO, James Nourse, in Milwaukee, WI. Nourse enjoyed collaborating with other CEOs and decided to start a peer group to share ideas and best practices. Soon there were dozens of groups throughout the Midwest.

When Bud signed on, TEC had around five hundred Chairs and ten thousand members in a dozen different countries. The United States had the highest concentration of TEC members. The corporate headquarters was in San Diego, CA.

Bud was invited to San Diego for a series of training classes to learn how to recruit members, form a group, and how to facilitate the monthly meetings and conduct the monthly one-to-one coaching sessions.

The training was rigorous and impactful. The other Chair hopefuls in Bud's training group included former CEO's, retired corporate executives, and business consultants like Bud. They came from all over the country. Over time, TEC had built a successful business model for how the groups were to operate and how the meetings were to be conducted. Bud was exposed to all this and much more over the course of three weeks of training spread over three months.

In the meantime, Bud was working hard to identify and recruit members for his first CEO group. It was not an easy sell asking busy executives to give up one day a month to join a new group chaired by a rookie Chair. Bud was provided a list of several hundred business owners in the metro Atlanta area by TEC's marketing department. He spent considerable time working that list and leveraging his existing relationships to find the right members for his new group.

Despite hearing more no's than yes's, Bud signed his first six members by June 2003 and was ready to have his first official meeting that month. This was a triumph for the new Chair and he was excited to finally get started.

Six years later, TEC rebranded itself and became Vistage. The new name came from two words. "Vista" suggests a look from above and "Advantage" suggests the benefit of having such a different perspective on your business and your life.

CHAPTER FOUR
THE GROUP

"No two minds ever come together without, thereby, creating a third, invisible, intangible force which may be likened to a third mind."
– Napoleon Hill

Peer groups or Mastermind groups back to the Greeks and Romans. The very first business peer group in the United States is believed to have been started by Ben Franklin. In addition to his political interests, Franklin was a successful business owner who enjoyed learning from other business owners in Philadelphia. He formed his first business peer group and called it a junta. The group met every week in a local pub where members discussed the many nuances of entrepreneurship late into the night.

One of the richest men in the United States in the late 19th century, Andrew Carnegie, was known for having his own Mastermind group that consisted of approximately 50 men who he met and spoke with regularly. Carnegie attributes much of his success in business and in life to this peer group.

Fifty years later, Napoleon "Think and Grow Rich" Hill said the following about such a Mastermind group:

"Economic advantages may be created by any person who surrounds himself with the advice, counsel, and personal cooperation of a group of men who are willing to lend him wholehearted aid, in a spirit of perfect harmony. This form of cooperative alliance has been the basis of nearly every great fortune."

Vistage groups come in all shapes and sizes. They can have as many as 20 members or as few as eight. The magic size seems to be between 12-18 members. Too few members and there is not enough "horsepower" in the group to discuss member issues. Too many members and there is not enough time for each member to get group attention and it gets increasingly hard for the Chair to facilitate the meeting effectively.

Vistage has several different types of groups. The traditional Vistage group is the **Chief Executive** group composed mostly of small business owners and operators. The company's range in size from less than $5 million in annual revenue to several hundred million dollars, with the average size around $20 million dollars and 40-50 employees.

The second type is the **Small Business** model. In these groups, the member's companies are smaller and generally have been in business for a shorter period of time. These companies tend to be more entrepreneurial with the CEO assuming a variety of different roles in the company.

The third type is the **Key Executive** group. This group is composed of company key executives such as the COO, the Vice-President, or even a business partner. This model was started with the intent of helping their CEO members grow and nurture future leaders within their respective companies.

The fourth Vistage group is the **Trusted Advisor** group. This group primarily includes individuals who work with CEOs such as accountants, attorneys, and financial advisors. Some of these members are soloists and some own their own practices. While these companies are much smaller than those of their CEO counterparts, they face some of the same issues that the larger companies do.

Bud Irvine's group, a Chief Executive group known on the roster as Vistage 526, meets every month for a full day. Each meeting is hosted by one of the members typically either at their office or a location of their choice such as a country club or a business club. In addition to the group meetings, the Chair meets individually with each member monthly for an executive coaching session known as the one-to-one.

The agenda for each group meeting remains mostly the same each month. There is typically a Vistage speaker presentation in the morning which lasts from two and a half to three hours. Vistage has one of the largest speaker bureaus in the country with more than 2000 speakers. Many of these presenters are professional speakers who also speak at national business conferences, write books, and work with Vistage size companies as consultants. Some of the speakers are retired Vistage members or Chairs who enjoy sharing their collective wisdom from years of executive experience. These are not college professors conveying management theory but rather are business practitioners sharing their real-life experiences.

The speaker presentations are meant to be interactive events as members engage with the speaker in more of a conversation than a one-way presentation. Speakers topics range from Sales and Marketing to Leadership, from Financial Management to Health and Fitness.

Members look forward to hearing Vistage speakers as an opportunity to learn new tools, new techniques, and new trends in an informal learning environment among other CEOs. They can freely ask questions of the speakers and discuss their own relevant experiences on each topic.

After the speaker's presentation, the members enjoy lunch and do a monthly check-in. The check-in is an opportunity for each member to update the group on what's happened in that members life and business and during the past thirty days. The group learns about new hires, recent business issues, and perhaps updates on the member's family.

After lunch, the member hosting the meeting makes a presentation. Typically, each member hosts and makes a host presentation once a year. The intent is for the member to provide the group with a complete overview of the business, including strategic plan, financials, an organizational chart, and any other high-level information that would be helpful to the others.

The host presentation serves dual purposes. First, it provides the group with a fundamental understanding of the member's business. Hence, when the member needs help with a specific business issue later in the year, the group has the proper context to provide needed consultation.

Second, the host presentation is also an opportunity for members to get a smart experienced group of business executives to look into their organizations and provide unbiased insights that the CEO might never get elsewhere. In this respect, by asking tough questions and providing powerful feedback the group is acting as the host member's own advisory group.

After the host presentation, the final portion of the day long meeting is the Executive Session in which the members have an opportunity to bring specific strategic decisions to the group for help in processing. Examples of such decisions might be a hiring or firing decision, a strategic growth decision about a new market or a new product offering, or possibly a financial issue. With the Chair facilitating, each issue discussion might take forty-five minutes to an hour. Each discussion ends with the member taking responsibility for some action in the weeks ahead with an expected follow-up report to the group in the next month's meeting.

Vistage 526 was formed by Chairm Bud Irvine in June 2003. It was fifteen years old this year. The group started with six members and grew to 16 within several years. During the economic recession of 2008-10, the group lost several construction business-related members due to the downturn. The size of the group fluctuated between ten and fourteen before returning to being full at sixteen in 2014.

CHAPTER 5
THE MEMBERS

"It is not the critic who counts. Not the man who points out how the strong man stumbles or where the doer of deeds could have done them better. The credit belongs to the man who is actually in the arena, whose face is marred by dust and sweat and blood, who strives valiantly, who errs, who comes short again and again, because there is no effort without error and shortcoming; but who does actually strive to do the deeds, who knows great enthusiasms, the great devotions, who spends himself in a worthy cause, who at best knows in the end the triumph of high achievement, and who at the worst, if he fails, at least fails while daring greatly, so that his place

shall never be with those cold and timid souls who neither know victory nor defeat."
– Theodore Roosevelt

Vistage members come from a variety of places. Some are referred by other members. Some are referred by Vistage headquarters. Bud Irvine had a significant professional network in his hometown of Atlanta and was fortunate to receive a number of referrals from that network.

Bud's typical member was an owner of a company with $15 million to $20 million in annual revenue and 50-75 employees. The company had been in business usually for 5-10 years prior to joining Vistage. Most of the companies were business-to-business (B2B) versus retail (B2C) or nonprofit organizations.

Most of the CEO's companies seemed to fall into one of two categories. Either the company was growing too fast and the CEO needed help managing the growth, or the company's growth had stalled and the CEO wanted help reinvigorating the growth of the business.

Members were interested in several factors when joining a peer group like Bud's. Many small business owners feel isolated in their role. They often do not have someone they can confide in about the business. They lack a confidant they can trust and share both the good and bad news relevant to the business.

Prospective members are also looking for growth opportunities for themselves. Many may have studied business in college or received good training with a large corporation early in their professional careers. Yet they feel that they are not quite equipped with the entrepreneurial tools or knowledge they need to lead the company to greater heights. They feel stuck.

New members also like the idea of having the added accountability of a peer group of CEOs to help them achieve the goals and strategies they have set out for themselves. They realize that they are accountable to themselves and their teams and they like the idea of adding an additional layer of accountability with their respective Vistage group.

In the Fall of 2018, Vistage 526 had fifteen members. One was an original member from 2003. Several had 8-10 years tenure with the group. Half had three to five years of experience with the group and there were three relatively new members.

Most Vistage groups are predominantly male. In some cases, that is a group or Chair decision. In Bud's case, it is more a factor of supply and demand. Fewer than 5 percent of the CEOs of small businesses in Atlanta are women and Bud's groups generally reflected that percentage. He did find that the more diverse the group, the more effective the group was in terms of both input and output.

The group was currently composed of the following members:

Ray Jernath. Ray was the longest tenured member of the group. He was a third-generation owner of a food processing business. Well educated, Ray had an arts degree from Emory University and an MBA from Georgia State University. Ray, a graduate of Leadership Atlanta, was very active in the Atlanta community having served on several local boards.

Cliff Junningham. Cliff was a corporate attorney with an Atlanta-based firm Turner Whitehead. He had been with the group for 10 years. He studied law at Vanderbilt University and also had an MBA from Georgia State University. In addition to having a keen understanding of the law, Cliff was a sharp business strategist and felt that one day he might be running his own company as the CEO.

Phil Balmer. Phil grew up in the Northeast, played college football and lacrosse, and then migrated to Georgia with his college sweetheart. Ten years ago he started, with a partner, an office furniture business with a business partner selling to large Atlanta Fortune 1000 companies and state universities. Phil joined the group about the same time as Cliff ten years ago.

Faheer Zaruqi. Faheer, a native of Pakistan, came to the United States to attend college on the West Coast. He loved aviation and started an airplane parts business from his garage in south Atlanta fifteen years ago. That business flourished and now sells almost twenty million dollars in airplane parts to airlines and foreign militaries worldwide. Faheer has considerable international trade experience and has traveled the globe many times over. He has three sons involved in his business and is eyeing a near-term exit strategy. Faheer has been with the group for eight years.

Theresa Mulsey. Theresa owns a large staffing agency in Atlanta specializing in blue collar placements. She has three office locations and her company has large contracts with several of the mega carpet manufacturers in Northwest Georgia. Theresa grew up in the staffing business and also had a business degree from Kennesaw State University. She is a seven-year Vistage member.

Carter Michaels. Carter works for a Berkshire Hathaway-owned company that distributes books and magazines to large retailers in the United States and Canada. Carter, an Atlanta native, attended Georgia Southern University. His first job was working in the warehouse at his current employer, eventually working his way up to president of this $2 billion dollar company. Carter joined the group six years ago and is one of the youngest members.

Dominique Patrick. Dominique is the president and CEO of Amhealth, a large Atlanta-based nonprofit that provides much needed prescription drugs to victims of a rare incurable disease. She has worked her entire career in healthcare and joined Amhealth 10 years ago as it's CEO. The operational company is very profitable, which then allows it to provide much-needed care for its sick clients. Dominique joined the group in 2012 and is eyeing retirement this year.

Trace Webster. Trace is a partner with Tenet Brasher, one of Atlanta's largest homegrown CPA firms. He heads up their real estate department. A Georgia native, Trace started off with one of the Big Five firms before joining Tenet Brasher. He graduated from the University of Georgia with a degree in accounting. He is an avid Bulldog fan and a five year Vistage member.

Tex Alexander. Tex is one of Atlanta's largest home builders. He played football at Georgia Tech and joined his father in the family-owned construction business right out of college. Over time, Tex has taken on more and more responsibility with the company and is now in charge of day-to-day operations. One of the younger members of the group, Tex joined Vistage four years ago after membership in a faith-based peer group.

Danny Goodall. Danny is the CEO of Goodall Pest Control. He attended the University of Georgia where he studied accounting and then attended UGA Law School. Rather than practice law, Danny joined his dad in the pest control business, and five years ago bought out his father. He is well-connected politically in the state of Georgia and there have been rumors of political ambitions in the near future for Danny. He has been a member for four years after relocating to Atlanta from Valdosta, GA.

Anthony (Tony) Barnett. Tony is a hired CEO at an Atlanta-based insurance company that specializes in high-risk reinsurance for the trucking industry. He is the only Black member of the group. Tony played football at Georgia Southern University before graduating and taking a job with the Insurance Commissioner in Georgia. He joined Summit Insurance ten years ago and worked his way up to CEO two years ago. Tony is a member of his church's vestry and also enjoys real estate investment. He joined the group in 2014.

Randy Sapatana. Randy owns an IT staffing business that specializes in placing technical experts with the Federal government. His business is headquartered in Macon, Georgia. Randy served in the U.S. Army for five years before leaving the service and starting his own business. Large government contracts have enabled his firm to grow rapidly and earn INC 500 status for three years running. At 33, Randy is the youngest member of his Vistage group, which he joined three years ago.

Will Kross. Will owns Melody Properties with 22 apartment complexes in Metro Atlanta. Another UGA grad, Will started in multi-family housing with his dad and then, after a difficult separation, started his own company. He has been very successful acquiring under performing properties and turning them into valuable investment properties. Will, one of the original members of the group, left for several years during the economic recession and then returned to the group in 2015.

Lacey Sutton. Lacey owns a marketing agency that specializes in digital communications. She was a past president of the Atlanta Marketing Association in Atlanta and is well respected in her industry. Lacey runs a boutique agency with twelve employees and several large retail clients. She recently turned down an opportunity to sell her business. Lacey is recently divorced and enjoys international travel. She is a three-year member.

Dave Borden. Dave is one of the original members of the Vistage group and is the president of the U.S. division of a large German paint company. He grew up in Boston, attended Northeastern University, and worked for General Electric for the first ten years of his career. Dave is well-read, a devout Catholic, and an avid golfer. He plans to retire in two years.

CHAPTER 6
PRE-MEETING

"It's Showtime, folks!"

– Joe Gideon, played by Roy Scheider, in the film All That Jazz

A Chair preparing for a Vistage meeting is like the producer of a Broadway play preparing for opening night.

The Chair must first determine which member will host the meeting. Every meeting is hosted by one of the group members. Hosting the meeting first entails providing the location for the group meeting. Most meetings are hosted either at the member's office in a boardroom or conference room or at a local country club.

The host provides a continental breakfast and lunch. Some meals are more elaborate than others. Sometimes members like to compete to see who can provide the most or least lavish meal to the group. The host must also be mindful of any dietary restrictions amongst the members. Bud Irvine encourages his hosts not to serve a hot lunch as it sometimes causes a comatose-like state for members mid-afternoon.

The host is also responsible for providing the group with a host presentation. This 30-to-45 minute presentation is meant to provide members with a foundational understanding of the member's business. It typically will include an overview of the company's strategic business plan, it's most recent financials, the organizational chart, and the member's exit strategy.

The host presentation is also an excellent opportunity for the member host to have a group of smart business CEOs dive into his or her business strategic domain and ask tough questions about the direction of the business, its capital investments, and their executive staffing.

For this meeting, Danny Goodall is the host at his Buckhead office. Danny has hosted the group several times before and always treats the group to good food, an accommodating meeting space, and a first-rate host presentation. Danny is exploring an acquisition of a competitor and is looking forward to getting some tough questions about that deal.

In addition to securing a meeting host, Bud Irvine is also responsible for lining up a Vistage Speaker for the meeting eight months a year. The other four month's meetings are full day Executive Sessions with no speaker. Today's meeting is a full day Executive Session. While the members will miss seeing a speaker, they also look forward to the opportunity to spend more time processing the member issues on this day.

Like a play's producer, Bud Irvine has a cast for this meeting and must determine what role each member will play. He has already determined that Danny Goodall will be the meeting host. Next, Bud needs to plan which members will bring issue discussions to the group. These will take up the majority of the group's time during this day.

For most Vistage members, the Executive Session portion of the meeting is the most interesting part of the day. A select number of the group members will either choose or be chosen to bring high-level strategic issues, usually decisions, to the group for discussion. Examples of such issues might be an executive hiring or firing, a business partner issue, an acquisition or a merger, or maybe a possible exit strategy.

Each issue's discussion usually takes 45-60 minutes. Over time, Vistage has developed a specific method for groups to process these issues and Bud received training on this process before launching his group. The process is as follows:

Step 1: The member presents a brief overview of their issue to the group verbally and, when possible in writing.

Step 2: The group, with the Chair facilitating, asks clarifying questions about the issue surfacing the facts and figures they need to know to help the member address this executive issue.

Step 3: The group next moves to asking tougher and more strategic questions about the decision. This often entails looking for any blind spots the member might have.

Step 4: The group now provides the member with their own perspective or experience on the issue as well as options moving forward.

Step 5: The member acknowledges the feedback and makes a commitment to the group on what will happen prior to the next group meeting.

Ten to fourteen days prior to the group meeting, Chairman Bud sends out a meeting notice to the group with the agenda, location, the host, and any other pertinent information. Members will respond with either their plans to attend or not. For this meeting, twelve of the members have responded with a "yes" to the meeting invite. Average group attendance is approximately eighty percent.

CE 526 Meeting Notice
Thursday, Feb 12, 2018
8:30 a.m. to 4:00 p.m.

Meeting Type: All Day Executive

Agenda
8:00 a.m.........Breakfast
8:30 a.m.........Welcome/Intros/Check-in
9:15 a.m.........Host Presentation
10:15 a.m.......Break
10:30 a.m.......Executive Session
12 p.m...........Lunch
1:00 p.m.........Executive Session (continued)
2:15 p.m.........Break
2:30 p.m.........Executive Session (continued)
3:45 p.m.........Wrap-up
4:00 p.m.........Adjourn

Host: Danny Goodall
Location: Goodall Pest Control
1455 Peachtree Road
Atlanta, Ga 30326
(404) 356-4275

The day before the group meeting, Bud checks in with the host to make sure he or she is ready. If there is a Vistage speaker, Bud will confirm with the presenter. Finally, Bud will send out a final email reminder to the group members the day before to make sure they know where the meeting is taking place and who the host is. The members appreciate this final reminder because it's easy to forget about the meeting details during the course of the month.

On the meeting day, Bud usually plans to arrive at the meeting location at least thirty minutes prior to when the members will start appearing. He likes to get there early to set out the member folders, make sure the room is set up properly, and make sure he is organized and prepared. Bud enjoys this little bit of quiet time before the organized chaos of the group meeting.

Members are assigned seats at the meeting. This is for two reasons. First, the fewer decisions a member has to make at the meeting the better. They spend their entire month making both important strategic decisions and smaller petty decisions. Bud has found over time that the members like having to make as few decisions as possible at the group meetings, starting with where to sit. Second, Bud likes to mix up the members each month. This gives the members the opportunity to get to know each other by not sitting next to the same person each month.

Every Vistage Chair is unique in how they facilitate their meetings, and the room set-up is no exception. Some Chairs like to practically wallpaper the walls of the room with flip chart paper containing famous quotes, group norms, discussion templates, and other group memorabilia. This creates a "clubhouse" effect for the members. Other Chairs prefer a simpler approach and leave the walls more barren.

On this occasion, Bud will have the meeting agenda on the wall along with a sign-in sheet where members check in with scores of 1-10 on their business and personal life the past 30 days. Bud finds this ritual helpful in that it forces the member to briefly reflect on the past month. It also serves as a transition for the arriving member from their commute to their active participation in that meeting.

Vistage Meeting **Sign-In** **V526…..2/12/18**				
Member (A/B/C)	**Business**	**Personal**	**Issue**	**Importance**
Danny	8	7	hosting	A
Ray	7	8	Exit strategy	A
Cliff	8	6	New offering	A
Phil	6	7	Biz partner	A
Faheer	7	9	A/R Collections	A
Theresa	8	8	Staffing	B
Dominique	9	8	Event	B
Trace	8	6	Kids school	B
Tex	6	9	CFO	A
Tony	8	9	Golf game	C

CHAPTER 7
MEETING DAY

"Your job as a leader is to be right at the end of the meeting, not at the beginning."
– Dave Cote, Honeywell

It's Thursday, Feb. 12th, 2018, meeting day for Vistage Chair Bud Irvine and his Vistage group. Bud has been a Vistage Chair for more than 15 years and by his count this is his 721st group meeting that he has chaired. Like the first seven hundred and twenty, this meeting will be like no other.

Bud starts the day with his customary walk with his dog Moe as he contemplates the beginning, middle and end of the upcoming meeting. He wondered both what could go right and what could go terribly wrong on this day? What will he be surprised by?

After his walk he journals briefly, as he does every day, and then gets ready to leave for his meeting. He packs his meeting bag with name tents, sign-in sheets, and member handouts. He takes one final look at his checklist to make sure he hasn't forgotten anything. After fifteen years of doing this work, there isn't anything he hasn't at one time forgotten to bring to a meeting including important articles of clothing.

Bud always likes to arrive at the meeting location early before the members and even sometimes even before the meeting host. Early morning Atlanta traffic is miserable and one never knows how long a crosstown commute might take. On this day, traffic seemed lighter than usual and he arrived on site right at seven-thirty a.m. for an eight-o-clock meeting start.

Danny Goodall's office is on the seventh floor of this Buckhead office building. Bud never enjoys lugging his meeting roller bag around these mammoth urban parking garages, and today was no exception. Upon arriving at Danny's office, Bud is greeted with cheer by Danny's admin Teri and directed to the board room. Danny is dropping off kids at school and should be arriving at the office very soon Teri explains.

The meeting room setup is often overlooked by group facilitators, but Bud is mindful of the importance of having the room arranged in just the right way. Rule number one is never to have empty chairs. Bud makes sure that there are just enough chairs for every member and no more. Empty chairs signify either poor planning or members choosing not to attend the meeting. Neither one is good.

Bud hangs the meeting agenda on one of the walls along with a great quote from the Chinese philosopher Sun Tzu:

"Strategy without tactics is the slowest route to victory. Tactics without strategy is the noise before defeat."

He then sets up the flip chart and makes sure the projector and screen are ready. Next, he hands out the monthly reading for each member. Bud takes great care each month to collect a dozen or so short articles on a variety of business topics for his members. He has found over time the members really look forward to receiving their monthly dose of business literature.

At 7:55 a.m., Bud checks to make sure breakfast is ready for the guests. Danny has just arrived and immediately darts back to his office to make several last minute edits to his host presentation. Finally, Danny taps his Spotify app on his cellphone and starts to play some jazz while the members begin to shuffle in.

Around 8 a.m., the members begin to arrive. It's February in Atlanta, and members arriving in heavy coats appreciate the warmth of Danny's office. Breakfast includes sweet rolls, bagels, and fresh fruit. Most importantly, there is hot coffee.

While many of the group members talk or email with each other between their group meetings, for most of them this is the only time they actually see each other. Warm hugs, firm handshakes, and big smiles greet each member entering the room. It's homecoming once a month.

Bud sees it as part of his responsibilities as a Chair to meet and greet every member as they arrive. He believes that everyone wants to feel welcome whether they are attending church, stepping into a store, or attending their monthly Vistage meeting. Bud provides each arriving member with a smile and a firm handshake.

Upon arrival, members find their designated seats. Over time Bud has found that the fewer decisions the members have to make on this day the better. They spend the majority of their waking time each month making big and little decisions at work and at home. On this day, they get a slight break on decision-making.

Bud also finds if he doesn't control the seating arrangement, members will tend to sit by the same person each meeting. He likes to change the seating each month so that the members get an opportunity to sit by different members each month and get to know each of them better.

CHAPTER 8
CHECK-IN...PART ONE

"Who in the world am I? Ah, that's the great puzzle."
– Lewis Carroll , Alice in Wonderland

Members are asked to check in prior to the start of the meeting. On the wall is the check-in sheet with four columns. The first column is for the member's name. The second column asks the members to rate their business life during the past 30 days on a scale of 1-10 where ten is fantastic and one is miserable. The third column asks for a similar rating on their personal life. The fourth column asks the members to identify the biggest decision they are working on currently in or outside of business. Examples might include a key hire or fire, a capital asset acquisition, or maybe a personal issue at home.

Bud has always found it interesting that newer members tend to be more honest in their responses on the check-in sheet. If business is average, they will put a five down in that column. Over time, more experienced members tend to give themselves a seven or eight in either column even if the "house is on fire". Bud is certain there is a good explanation for this phenomenon from a behavioral psychologist.

The check-in sheet is very important to Bud as a Chair because it gives him some sense of each member's status at the beginning of the meeting. Any scores less than 5 will get his attention either on a one-to-one basis or with the group.

Bud notices that on this day most of the members ratings are 7s and 8s. There are several outliers, however. Phil Balmer has a five for business and a "partner" issue. Tex Alexander has a four for personal and has written "health issues" next to the score. Lacey Sutton has written a four for business and added "terrorist" under the issue column. Bud takes note of each of these and immediately assumes that there will be no shortage of issue discussions in today's Executive Session.

As members arrive, Bud senses that most are in good spirits. Ray Jernath was the first member to arrive and he finds his designated place at the conference table and then goes in search of breakfast. Trace Webster is next to arrive. He gets a warm welcome from Ray and host Danny Goodall. Theresa Mulsey arrives about 8:15 a.m. and she is a bundle of positive energy as she gives warm hugs to everyone in the group.

The members in this group enjoy seeing each other on meeting day. Many of them have been in this group for five to ten years and have gotten to know each other well. Several of them also get together outside of the monthly meetings for golf, lunch, or just drinks after work.

At 8:30 a.m., Bud Irvine calls the meeting to order. One member, Carter Michaels, is out of town and will miss the meeting. Two members, Faheer Zaruqi and Randy Sapatana both have long commutes and are running late.

"Welcome Vistage 526 members," Bud states firmly to the group.

"Welcome to our February meeting," Bud continues. "We have a very busy agenda today and we will get started now."

Bud then reviews the meeting agenda. First up on the meeting agenda is the member check-in. This is an opportunity for each member to share significant events, both business and personal, from the past thirty days. It's a warm-up exercise that also helps everyone engage in the meeting and disengage from whatever matters they were involved in prior to the meeting.

Next on the agenda for that day is the host presentation. Today, Danny will present his business plan for 2018, his year-to-date financials, and share his plans for a potential acquisition. He will also take questions from the group and receive in-depth feedback on the state of his business.

There will be a break for lunch and the remainder of the day will be spent in Executive Session processing any significant strategic issues any of the members may have for the group. There will be a closing exercise for the group and then will adjourn by 4 p.m.

"Danny, any housekeeping the group needs to be aware of?" Bud asks his meeting host.
Danny is caught looking at his cellphone and abruptly looks up and responds, "Plenty of breakfast in the kitchen. Men's and women's bathrooms down the hallway. No codes necessary. Wi-Fi information is on the whiteboard."

Bud always hopes for no Wi-Fi connection as the members do not need any help accessing their cellphones. It's an unneeded distraction for members who are already easily distracted.

This group, in general, is pretty good about not using their devices during the meeting. Bud will remind them from time to time to keep them off the conference table if at all possible. Several months ago the group had a speaker who cited research suggesting that just having sight of your cellphone causes participants in a meeting to lose as much as 50 percent of their attention to the speaker.

"Thanks Danny," says Bud. "Let's get started with our check-in now. Three 'Goods and One 'Bad' the past thirty days."

Bud uses a variety of different check-ins with his groups. This one, "Three goods and a bad" came from a child psychologist he met several years ago. She said that she used this check-in to start every client session. The intent is to shift the mind from believing that there are more "bads" in the world than "goods." In this case, three times more "goods."

Bud starts the check-in with Ray Jernath. "Three goods," Ray says. "The first good is I finally got our oldest meat processor working again. It had been down for two weeks. Real pain in the ass. The second good is we have started selling beef patties to the new baseball stadium. Big first order."

Ray's company is a third-generation ground beef processing business. Most of the burgers in Atlanta restaurants originate in his 50-year old facility located near Grant Park by the old federal prison.

"Third good is that I had a great trip to New York City for the weekend. Visiting friends. We saw 'Hamilton'...again," Ray smiled as he shared this with the group. He loved attending shows, and this was his third visit to see Hamilton.

"The bad is my cousin Terry. He's my operations manager. We're still not on the same page. He pissed me off last week when he decided not to work for several days. I had to open and close both days. I'm getting too old for this bs," Ray shared disgustingly.

Cliff Junningham was next to report. "Great month," he declared to the group. "I had one big acquisition that finally closed. Damn lender kept changing the terms on the financing. The buyer and seller finally got the deal done with a little help from their attorney." Cliff grinned as he shared this with the group as he knew that it was his own behind-the-scenes ma-neuvering that got this deal to the finish line.

"I also added a new outside general counsel client this month. This new marketing program is finally producing some results for me," Cliff stated. The group had been hearing about this new practice offering for several months and Cliff had begun to show some exasperation because there had been limited success with the roll-out so far.

"And the girls are doing great in school," Cliff added. He was married and had two teenage girls ages 11 and 14. "Kate, our oldest, made the school play and Laura, our youngest, is playing soccer."
"Cliff, you're no help with either one of those are you?" Phil Balmer shouted out to his friend sitting across the room. "You can't sing and god help you if you tried to run up and down a soccer field."

Cliff smiled as his friend was enjoying jabbing him so early in the meeting. "You may be right on both counts Phil," Cliff responded. "Thanks for the positive reinforcement."
"And the bad?", Chair Bud asked Cliff while trying hard to redirect the conversation.

"The bad is I lost my car," said Cliff. "I parked it in the building lot when I got to work last Wednesday. I wasn't really paying attention to which floor I parked on. Lots on my mind that morning. When I walked out at lunch to run a few errands, the car was gone. Or maybe I should say I couldn't find it. I looked everywhere. I even reported it to the building security. And then, I realized I was looking in the wrong parking lot. I was in the Green lot."

"Clearly a senior moment counselor,"piped in Theresa Mulsey, who could hardly help herself from smiling.
"Have you considered a driver Cliff?" asked Trace Webster, unable to resist a poke at his friend.

"Sounds more like 'Driving Miss Daisy' to me," asserted Tex Alexander, grinning from ear to ear.

Cliff, realizing that he probably should have kept this story to himself, looked sheepishly at the group and hoped that Bud would move to the next member.

"Phil, you're next," said Bud looking at the forty-five year old former college athlete.

"How about we just stay with Cliff a bit longer", Phil responded. "My guess there's more to this story".

"I think Cliff is done for now Phil," Bud said. "You're next".

"I'll start with the bad", Phil began. "My business partner has gone awol again. No word from him now in ten days. Part of me is worried and part of me is actually somewhat relieved."
Phil and his partner Steve Cave started the office furniture business almost 15 years ago. They were friends and Steve's dad, who owned the business and sold it to them for a nominal amount. Early on, the partnership flourished with both partners making sales and overseeing day-to-day operations. Over time, Steve's role diminished to just being an account rep and Phil became the CEO of the fast growing enterprise.

"Is anyone looking for him?" asked meeting host Danny Goodall. "Maybe this is a blessing in disguise? That guy has been missing from the business for a while, hasn't he?"

"Yes he has, and this time I am worried about him," Phil said, sensing that maybe there may be more to this story than the group had heard before. "He's been under a lot of stress at home with a broken marriage and kids from two different mothers. I think he may have left town this time. Not a good situation."
"I do have some good news though," Phil added. "The new sales VP is a keeper I think. She's rallied the sales team and we're seeing good results. We have also been shortlisted on a large state contract for Georgia Tech's new space research building that could be huge. I have been working all week on that proposal."

"Phil, can you handle that large of a deal?" asked Tony Barnett, taking his eyes away from his cellphone and focusing directly on Phil. "A contract like that could bury you just as easily as it could be a revenue boom. Better to die from starvation than choke from indigestion," he added.

"I'll take indigestion all day long," Randy Sapatana shouted from the far side of the meeting room. "That whole starving thing is overrated," he suggested to Phil and the group with a slight grin.

Just taking his place at the table is late-arriving Faheer Zaruqi. "Faheer, you're next," directed Bud. "Three goods and one bad".

Faheer settled into his seat and deliberated for a brief moment. "Let me catch my breath please," he responded. "Traffic from Peachtree City was a disaster. Two wrecks on the interstate and I was almost the third."

" The first good is that I am here safely," Faheer said. "The second good is that sales year-to-date have exceeded last year. The boys are really working hard."

The boys Faheer referenced are his three sons who all work in the export airplane parts business.

"With any luck I may just achieve my goal of exiting this crazy business in the next three years," Faheer added. The group had heard about this exit strategy for most of the ten years Faheer had been a member of the group. There has always been some doubt as to whether he truly wanted to exit the business or if he could pull off a successful exit strategy.

"My third good is a new bank deal. Finally happened. I'm so tired of talking with all of these bankers. All promising us lots of money and then tying up our accounting folks with more paperwork than they can possibly withstand. The deal with South Bank is done and our line of credit is back."

"And the bad?" asked Bud, trying to keep the dialogue moving.
"The bad is the lawsuit," Faheer shared with a groan. "This lawsuit with our Indian trading partner may never go away. I'll take it to my grave."
Faheer and his sons had entered into a trading agreement with an Indian partner over a year ago with hopes of establishing a sales office in New Delhi. After six months, there were no sales and Faheer decided to exit the partnership. The trade partner has sued the company for over $100,000 in expenses related to opening the sales office.

"How much will they settle for?" asked Trace Webster. "They can't possibly believe that you're on the hook for the whole amount can they?"

Faheer responded that "Our counsel has offered $50K and that's all I'm willing to spend. This man is a crook and I refuse to be a hostage in this game of his."

Faheer was getting more frustrated as the conversation continued, so he got up from the table to get some hot tea to settle his nerves.

"Theresa, you're next" Bud said as he continued the group check-in. Theresa had missed the past two meetings and the members were anxious to get caught up.
"Sorry fellas for missing December and January," Theresa shared remorsefully. "We were at a big staffing conference in Orlando the first month and I can't even remember where I was last month. It's been crazy."
"Lots of good news to share," Theresa continued. "We made the Best Places to Work list in Atlanta Magazine. For a staffing agency, that's a big deal. We also got to the next round on a mega proposal from Allied Carpet in their new plant in Calhoun. Over 500 new hires over the next twelve months. Those old boys are watching every nickel and dime on this one. And lastly, both girls got accepted into Cobb Baptist school for the Fall. That's going to cost us a bundle."

"The bad," Theresa continued, "Jimmy, my favorite husband, has gotten a job offer down in Valdosta with a credit union. They want him to be president."

"Will that mean a move for you?" asked Dominique Patrick.

"I'm not sure at this moment," responded Theresa. "I hate the thought of dragging both kids out of school and down to Valdosta. I could still run the business from there. I might need to commute several days a week. It's a great career opportunity for Jimmy. I don't know…", Theresa's voice trailed off as she pondered the thought of another move.

"Dominique, you're next," Bud announced. Dominique Patrick looked startled as she was peeking at her cell phone when the Chair called her name.

"Sorry Bud", she responded. "I have a little issue at home I am dealing with. What are we doing?"

"Hello Dominique," chimed in Trace Webster grinning slyly. "Welcome to the meeting."

Dominique hastily put her phone down and smiled at Trace. 'Thanks, Trace. Wait until you have screaming kids at home. Our daycare provider is stuck in traffic and my husband is about to explode if he doesn't get relief."

"Okay Bud, what are we doing?" asked Dominique.

"Three goods and a bad," replied Bud. "And I think we already have the bad," he added.
"That's more like three bads," Dominique quickly added.

"Okay, first good is we have completed a state audit and we passed with flying colors. Our CPA firm did a great job along with our accounting team. Thank god we only have to do this every two years. What a mess!"

"My second good was the golf tournament last month. We raised over a hundred thousand dollars in one day. We got lucky with the weather. I want to thank Danny and Tex for playing."

"Welcome, Dominique," piped in Danny. "Tex may have the worst golf swing of any CEO I know. I carried him all day long." Danny grinned at Tex and got a big smile back from his friend.

"My last good is my last hire. I finally found a development person I can work with. He worked hard on this golf tournament and has really ignited our fundraising this year. We got lucky on this one."

"And Bud you're right on the bad. This whole day-care situation, particularly in the morning, has been a disaster," added Dominique looking quite frustrated. "I may need to find a way to work more from home until we can figure out a better solution."

"Thanks Dominique," responded Bud. "Trace, you're up next."

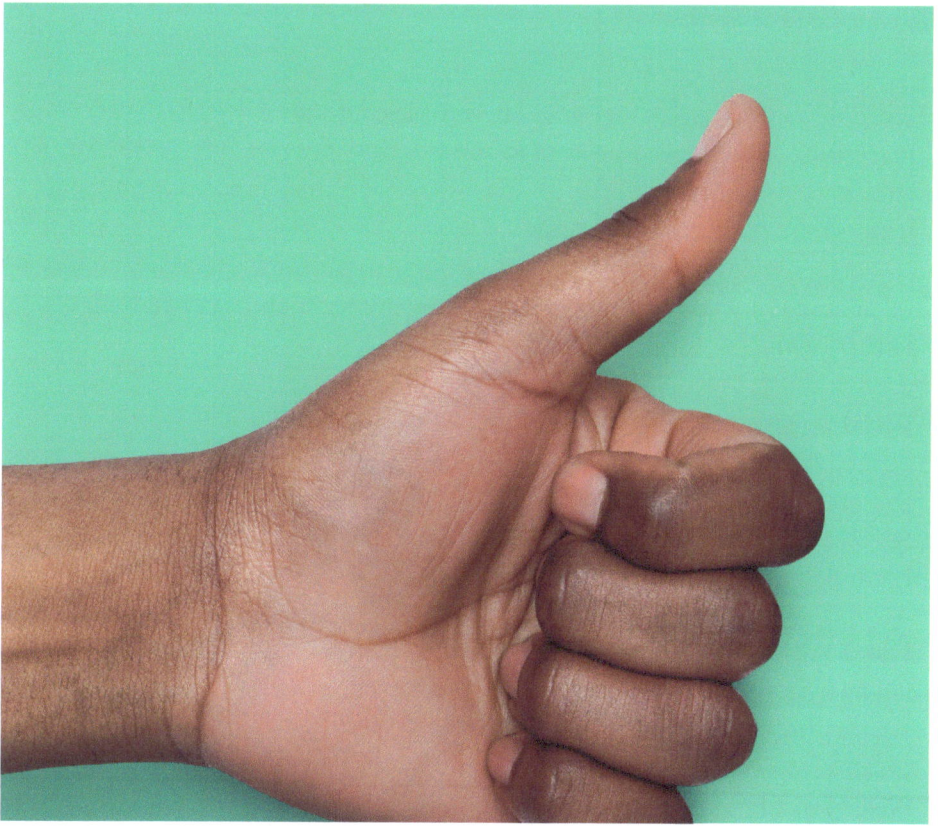

CHAPTER 9
CHECK-IN...PART TWO

"Knowing yourself is the beginning of all wisdom."
– Aristotle

Trace Webster was a five-year member of the group and never enjoyed this portion of the meeting. He was one of the more private members of the group and always thought this part of the meeting took too much time.

"Three goods? Tax season, tax season, and tax season," Trace shared. "I love it. Lots of work. Staying busy. Bad? Tax season. We're behind schedule. Not enough help. New tax laws are causing chaos on our team, but we're good."

"Trace, is my return on top of your desk?" asked Tony Barnett in a teasing voice. "Don't tell me we're going after another extension this year. I should be a priority."

"Tony, we have actually just passed your file directly to the IRS. Why waste time? Those boys should be contacting you any day now," Trace responded with a sly grin. "You will look good in stripes behind bars. I warned you against those offshore accounts."

Bud always enjoyed hearing the bantering among members and believed it spoke to their closeness.

"Tex, you're on next," asserted Bud. "Tell us about the last 30 days."

Tex Alexander was in his mid-30's. He was carrying about ten pounds more than he did in his football playing days at Georgia Tech and he had been quiet so far this morning.

"Best news is that dad and mom are out of the country for a month. We tend to fight less the farther removed dad is from the business," Tex shared with the group.

"Have you considered a space flight?" asked Will Kross with a smile on his face. "That would tie him up for years at a time."

"I have," responded Tex. "I'm not sure the aliens would put up with that much longer than I have."

"Number 2 good news is that we have purchased a beautiful piece of land for development just north of the lake. A 100 acres. It was a steal. It's been held up in court for years and just came on the market. We snatched it up before anyone else could see it."

"Third? Crap, I don't know. Tech football has a new coach. Good guy. It was time for a change. Money stopped coming into the program with the old coach."

"And the bad news? Well, there's no change there. My CFO is at it again. He's now gone for a two week vacation. Didn't tell anyone. Just gone. Missing in action. If his name wasn't on every document we have signed the past ten years, I would fire that sob tomorrow. Pain in the ass…"

"Tex, he must have compromising pictures of you in college. You've been pissed at that guy for years," shouted Dave Borden from across the room. "And they're not flattering photographs, I might add."

"Dave, first of all, all my pictures are flattering and secondly, I will remove that ***hole sooner than later. I will promise the group." Tex responded quickly. His demeanor changed noticeably the more he thought about his endangered CFO.

Danny Goodall was next to check-in. As the meeting host, Danny had been taking note of the number of members in attendance so far and those not here yet. He also noticed that the coffee in the kitchen had gotten low and he shot a quick text to his assistant to make a fresh pot.

"This has been a good month, fellas," Danny began. "Four of five of our markets are on budget year to date. I may have to make a move on one of my area managers. He's not quite making numbers this year. We are looking at a small acquisition in Atlanta. No big deal. A soloist with no future. And the last good is that UGA basketball season is almost over. What a disaster this season has been!", Danny's voice trailed off as he lamented about his alma mater's state of affairs.

"And the bad Danny?" Bud asked.

"I'll save the details for my host presentation, but I need to hire a No. 2 sooner than I thought. I've got too many direct reports and it's time to add another layer in my organization."

"Why's that bad?" asked Will Kross from across the table.

Danny's face turned more serious as he responded,"It's just going to be a pain in the ass to find the right person and then figure out exactly what that role looks like. But I know it's time."

"It's past time Danny," shouted Lacey Sutton from across the room. "You've been talking about this for a year. What are you afraid of?"

Danny grinned for a second as he realized that Lacey was right. "You're worse than my wife Lacey. She says the same thing. Time to move forward."

"I'll take that as a compliment Danny," Lacey responded with a grin.

"Alright, let's keep moving folks," Bud told the group. "Time is slipping away. Tony, you're next."

Tony Barnett had been enjoying the group banter. He tended to be more reserved than some of the other members.

"It's been a crazy month. The insurance commissioner has been on us about several of our newest products. Too much risk, he says."

Tony had actually worked for the Georgia Insurance Commissioner right out of college and knew how that office operated.

"We are also looking at a possible acquisition. A small carrier out of Macon. They're in several markets we have not been able to penetrate. They're smart guys. Asking for a boatful of money. I may need some help from the group on this one," Tony shared.

"Third good is my oldest daughter. She's engaged. Nice guy. Wedding in June. I'm passing the hat at lunch for donations for the reception. This one is going to set me back at least $50K. Who's going to help me?" Tony smiled as he looked around the room knowing that several of the members had recently had expensive weddings and had complained about the costs associated with those events.

"The bad is my damn golf game," Tony growled to the group. "Even Danny took my money last week on the 18th hole. Lessons, new clubs, even some physical therapy; and my game is still shit."

"Tony, you're working too much," shouted Tex Alexander to his friend. "Your golf game would improve dramatically if you left your cell phone at the office. It's all about concentration buddy. You have none." Tex smiled wide as he berated Tony.

Randy Sapatana was next and he was just arriving at the meeting. As he took his seat he started.

"Sorry kids. Traffic was a disaster. Waze told me ninety minutes from Macon and it took me two hours. What have I missed?" Randy looked around the room.

"You missed breakfast Randy," yelled Phil Balmer from the head of the table. "Best Chick-fil-A biscuits I ever had. I had the last one brother."

Randy looked at Phil with a bit of disdain and started his check-in.

"Six new placements for us this month. Great news. Army folks are finally starting to move a little faster with our guys," Randy shared with the group. His staffing business had experienced some slowness recently as the Army was wrestling with budget issues.

"The terrorist we hired at Fort Hood was asked to leave his assignment," Randy explained.

"You mean a real terrorist Randy?" asked Tex Alexander with concern.

"No, just a young guy with a bad attitude. Not a good fit for that office. We may try to place him somewhere else. He needs the cash and we need the recurring revenue."

"Last good is we took another family trip to Disney last weekend. Great time. The park was not as crowded as usual."

"They knew you were coming Randy," said Trace Webster with a grin. "Your family monopolizes the whole park one ride at a time."

Randy smiled at Trace. He took his family to Walt Disney World at least six times a year and he was on a first name basis with many of the ride attendants.

"And the bad?" asked Bud of Randy.

"The bad, besides today's commute, is my wife's health. She's doing better but not quite back to where she was before the surgery. Slow recovery which means I'm doing a lot of kids' stuff around the house. Not my deal but I'm doing the best I can."

"Randy, one less Disney trip and you could afford help with that you know," asserted Tex Alexander with a wide grin on his face.

"Will, you're next," Bud noted from across the room. "Tell us about the last thirty days."

Will was one of the quieter members of the group and careful with his words.

"Multi-family housing is red hot right now friends," he started. "We're above ninety percent occupancy at each of our properties including the dog down in Fayette County we've been struggling with for years. Each property's cash is flowing really well.

"The second good piece of news is that we finally re-financed the Cobb County property. That was a long drawn out affair between the bank going through a merger, the feds dragging their feet, and the county changing their requirements on us mid-stream. I earned my pay on this one."

Will grew up in the apartment business and knew it better than anyone in the Atlanta market. He was a stickler for details and could get buried in spreadsheets for days at a time.

"My third good is my son Barry. Starting pitcher for his high school base-ball team. He's really worked hard this year," Will shared with the group before being interrupted by Dave Borden.

"Will, the real feat there is the fact that you don't have an athletic bone in your body and that kid is a phenom. Momma must have been quite an athlete in her day."

Dave enjoyed ragging Will when he could, and this was no exception.

"The bad news," Will continued, "is that dad and I are still not speaking. Not a word for three months. My stepmom has tried to negotiate a truce between us and there's no telling when we might speak again. Too much bad blood. He tried to screw me on that last deal and I caught him."

"Easter dinner should be a real joyful event in the Kross family," Phil Balmer barked as he was grabbing his second cup of coffee. "Can't wait to be a fly on the wall for that one."

"There will be no breaking of bread for us anytime soon," responded Will. "That SOB won't get near my kids anytime soon if I can help it."

"Lacey, you're next," said Bud, noticing that Will's face was getting redder the more he spoke.

Lacey had been quiet so far this morning but perked up quickly at the mention of her name. She was one of the more popular members in the group.

"Let's start with the bad news boys," she smiled as she looked around the room.

"We lost the whale. Huge account. Hooked it last Fall and never quite got it on the boat. Not a good fit. And you know what? I knew it on the first date. First meeting with the CEO. He was an oddball. But boy did we need that extra cash. Couldn't say no to this one. We hired a new account exec just to babysit this one. I should have trusted my instincts on this one."
Lacey's big smile turned to a frown as she shared her whale story. This was not the first time the group had heard the misfortunes of securing a very large new piece of business only to lose it on account of a misalignment of core values.

"Enough bad news," Lacey continued, "Good news number one is that the divorce is final. Papers signed. We're actually talking to each other for the first time in months and both girls seem to be okay with the living arrangements."

Lacey and her ex-husband had been business partners at one time and then the relationship began to go sour. The group had front row seats to a bad marriage that played out for several years.

"Next, while the last buyer changed his mind we may have another agency interested in merging with us. Might be a good fit."

"Do you really need to be looking at another marriage?"asked attorney Cliff Junnigham. Cliff had been her legal counsel in several past deals.
"I know, Cliff. It may be a little soon for me. Let's talk off-line."

"Last bit of good news for me is that my Italy trip is booked. Three days in Rome followed by a week at the Amalfi Coast. It will be heaven with everything I've been through lately. The girls will be back in school and I will be off in paradise." Lacey now was back to a full smile on her face and the group was smiling with her.

"Dave, we have saved the best for last. Three goods and a bad my friend," stated Bud.

"I hate going last," said Dave. "I've been editing my notes here now for the past thirty minutes. I'm up to seven goods and three bads. Where should I start?"

"The condensed version would be best Dave," Bud responded. "We're close to an hour into the meeting and still checking in.

"Okay, I'll be quick. First good is that my golf handicap is down two strokes the past ninety days. That's quite a feat for me."

"Not bad considering you're now spending more days on the golf course than in your office Dave," suggested Tony Barnett from across the table. "If you could putt, you'd be even more dangerous."

Dave Borden took his golf game and his business quite seriously.

"Tony, I believe you still owe me a hundred dollars from the last scramble we played in. How was my putting that day friend? Dave responded with a grin towards his golfing buddy.

"Second good is that we have an opportunity for a joint venture in Chile. Small distributor but a great chance to break into the Latin American market. I better start working on my Spanish."

"Last good news is that my youngest daughter is engaged. Great guy. A financial advisor with Morgan Stanley."

"I don't believe that I have seen my wedding invitation Dave," host Danny Goodall inquired. "That should be quite a shindig."

"No kidding," Dave responded. "Easily a hundred K before I'm done. I'll be passing a hat before the end of today's meeting fellas. Be generous."

Bud smiled as he saw the members engage with each other. The check-in was completed and it was time for a quick break and then the host presentation.

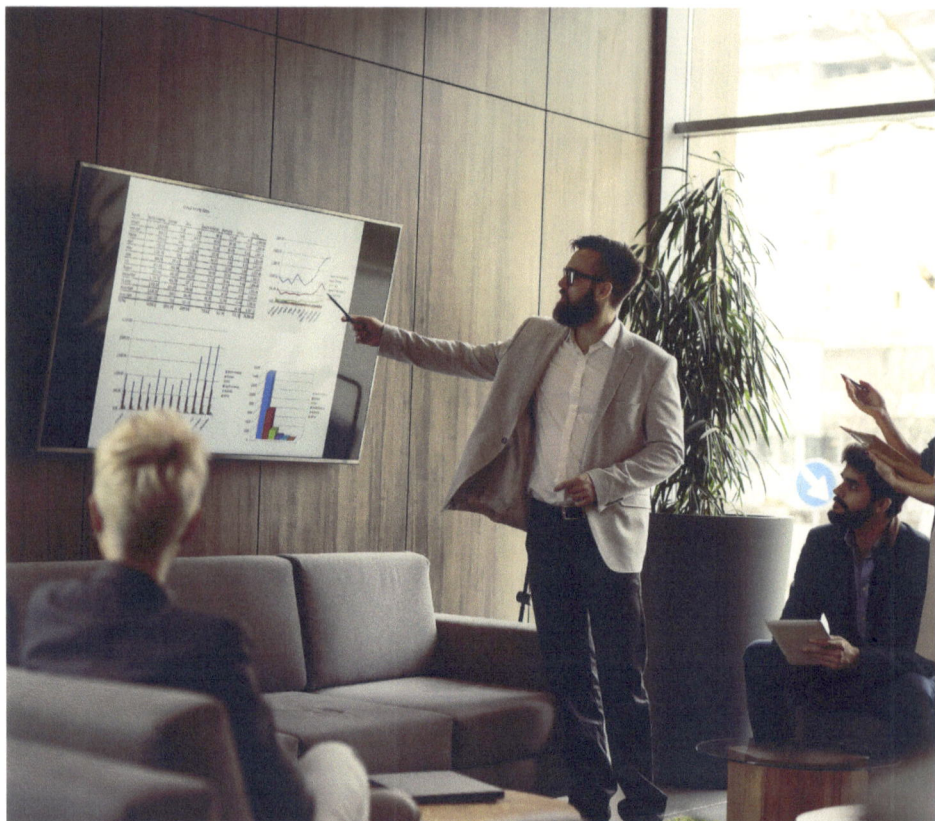

CHAPTER 10
THE HOST PRESENTATION...
ONE-PAGE BUSINESS PLAN

*"A good speech should be like a woman's skirt;
long enough to cover the subject and short
enough to create interest."*
– Winston S. Churchill

The host presentation is always one of the favorite parts of the Vistage meeting for Bud as well as many of the members. It's a great opportunity for the group to take a deep dive into the host member's business to better understand the strategic intent, the financial performance, and the organizational design of the business.

The only person who does not always look forward to the host presentation is the host.

First, it requires hours of preparation updating the business plan, reviewing the financials, and organizing a coherent PowerPoint presentation. Secondly, it was a nervous time for the host as they expose their business to the group for tough questions and sometimes brutally candid feedback.

A typical one-hour host presentation might include any of the following elements:
- Historical background on the firm
- Brief overview of the company's offering and it's market
- A one-page business plan highlighting the mission, vision, core values, and long- and short-term goals and strategies
- Recent financials including either charts or financial statements or both
- Current organizational chart
- The member's annual business and personal goals
- A snapshot of the member's behavioral profile
- A glimpse of the member's life outside of work including family, hobbies, etc.
- Q&A from the group and a round of feedback from the members

Our host this day, Danny Goodall, had done several host presentations over his four-year tenure with the group, so he skipped over the history of the firm and the overview of the company's service offering to save time for the other portions of his presentation. He was anxious to receive good feedback from the group on his one-page business plan, the financials, and his organizational chart.

Danny had spent several hours earlier in the week on his presentation in addition to an hour this morning touching up several portions of the powerpoint. He felt both ready and a bit nervous about what was about to take place.

2019
One-Page Business Plan
Goodall Pest Control
Our Mission
Create safety and peace of mind for all of our stakeholders
Our Vision
We dominate the markets we serve

Our Core Values
Safety • Growth • Tell the truth • Do your job • Support the team

Three-Year Goals
1. 15 percent annual revenue growth and 15 percent annual net profit (EBITDA)
2. Become a "Best Place to Work" in Georgia
3. Invest $1 million to accelerate the use of technology in our company

2019 Goals
1. $15 million in revenue & 15 percent net profit
2. Reduce employee turnover by 20 percent and improve our onboarding process
3. Open one new market and introduce one new service offering.

Key Strategies
1. Redesign the org chart and hire a COO
2. Create a KPI and an employee career path for every team member
3. Explore the use of Artificial Intelligence in our business

---

Danny started with his one page business plan (1PBP). The group had been exposed to a variety of 1PBP formats by different Vistage speakers through the years. Some formats were more extensive and more complicated than others. This group liked simplicity and clarity. Danny's seemed to reflect both properties in his plan as he began to share it with the group.

"Boys, here it is" started Danny. "Our updated 2019 One Page Business Plan. Read it and weep. My executive team has spent a lot of time on this plan this year and we feel good about where we are. Pretty self-explanatory.

What questions do you have?"
Chair Bud Irvine started the questioning. "Danny, it might be helpful to provide the group with some definitions. What do you mean by mission, vision, and core values?"

"No problem Bud. The mission is our 'why'. The reason the business exists. Our core purpose. For us, it's all about safety and peace of mind for our external customers and for our employees as well."

"We really gained clarity around our 'why' after watching Simon Sinek's TED Talk on the subject. Very illuminating. In his latest book, "The Infinite Game," the author refers to it as your "Just Cause". Something worth fighting for.

Danny continued."In the TED Talk, Sinek says that 'people don't buy what you sell, they buy why you sell it.' In our case, we are crazy passionate about our stakeholders feeling safe in their homes and in their jobs."

"The vision is our long-term destination. This is where we expect to end up when we are done. The peak of success. Right now we are working hard to be the number one, two, or three in each of our markets in terms of revenue generated. Our vision is to be numero uno in each market."

"I was first introduced to this idea of vision when I first read Steven Covey's best-selling book 'Seven Habits of Highly Successful People'. My favorite 'habit' was 'Start with the end in mind.' I have always felt that as an organization, we needed to define what that end looks like. Ultimate success. Jim Collins calls it your BHAG. Big Hairy Audacious Goal."

"Hey Danny," Dave Borden spoke out from the other side of the room. "I remember we had that speaker James Newton say something powerful to us several years ago about vision. I still have it written down in my notebook." Dave showed the group his page.

"In the absence of a clear vision, people tend to recreate their past."

"Thanks Dave," responded Danny. "There was a time that I had a lot of my people recreating their past with us and it wasn't good."

Danny moved on to the next line in his plan. "The core values are a handful of guiding principles by which our company navigates. They define appropriate behavior for our employees. Non-negotiables. Our intolerables. If violated, employees are at risk of losing their jobs."

"Danny, how did you arrive at each of these?" asked Ray Jernath. "I'm impressed!"

"We had an off-site last Fall. Brought in an outside facilitator. We spent an entire day just getting started on each of these. The mission we kind of already knew. The vision was really tough. We had a hard time getting a consensus on this one. Lots of fierce conversations amongst my executive team."

Danny continued, "The core values were a little easier. I remember a quote from best-selling author Jim Collins who said, 'You don't develop core values...you discover them'. So we just spent time talking about what was most important to us as a team in terms of our values and this is what we arrived at."

"Hey Danny, how do you use these core values within the company?" asked Cliff Junningham with a puzzled look on his face. "We did this once at the firm. Came up with five or six values, wrote them down, and then never saw them again. They disappeared. How do you prevent that from happening here?"

"Cliff, that happened to us the first time we did this. We hired a high-priced consultant to help us. He surveyed the employees and we came up with these aspirational values that were more what we wanted to become and less who we were at the time. They never got traction within the company. They're gone."

"This time it's different. First, we use these core values extensively in the interviewing process. Every prospective new hire has to be completely aligned on at least three of the five values, somewhat synced on a fourth, and we will allow one miss as long as it's not a glaring misalignment. As a result, we have found our hiring practices have improved five-fold just from that one practice."

"To quote Jim Collins again, he said you can't expect employees to buy into your core values, you have to hire individuals who already possess these beliefs."

Danny continued: "Next, we spend a lot of time in almost every meeting reinforcing these values. I look for people demonstrating them and I take time to recognize them. When something goes bad, I try to tie that negative event to a core value whenever possible. We also use these core values in all of our team coaching sessions and performance reviews."

"You would think people would get tired of hearing about our core values, but they don't. In fact, now my employees are starting to build them into their day to day conversations at work. I hear them all the time. It's great."

"Danny, how long are these first three things good for?" asked Phil Balmer sitting next to Danny. He was referring to Danny's mission, vision, and core values.

"One hundred years or more" responded Danny. "Very unlikely that they will change over time. Like the foundation of a home. You may make changes to the exterior or interior of your house, but the foundation stays the same."

"And what is your role with all this stuff?" asked Faheer from the front of the room.

"Bud keeps telling me that I am the CMO," Danny responded, "that stands for Chief Meaning Officer. I am responsible for making sure all three of these - the mission, vision, and core values - stay alive in perpetuity. That also makes me the enforcer."

"What's interesting," Danny continued, "is that we have seen several very positive results from having these three things.

"First, decision-making within the company has gotten much easier. When someone comes to me with a tough question, I just say 'How do our core values speak to this decision?' In fact, I am now less involved in a lot of decision-making than I have ever been."
"Second, since announcing our strategic intent, we have lost several employees who I think just didn't feel like they fit into this new strategic initia-

tive. They essentially fired themselves. Made it easy for us."

"And last, I believe that the employees who have chosen to stay are ten times more engaged in their work. It now has a different level of meaning to them. It's powerful. In fact, we have gotten more employee referrals for new employees the past six months than we ever have. People are now seeking us out for work."

"Danny." Phil Balmer had raised his hand to be recognized by the host, "How do you arrive at the three year goals? They seem very ambitious big guy." Phil had a fun grin on his face as he posed his question.

"They are ambitious Phil," responded Danny. "They have to be. These are stretch goals for us. They do make me a little uncomfortable when I think about them."

"In order to determine our revenue growth, we used a tool that Bud introduced to me called Sustainable Growth Rate (SGR)*. Using our projected net profit, our debt to equity ratio, and our variable asset percentage, the SGR calculates for us what a safe rate of growth is over the next twelve months. In our case the number was 15 percent. It doesn't mean that we can't grow faster, but we would do so knowing that we are taking on a significant risk load. We've been using SGR for years and it has been very helpful and accurate in projecting our revenue growth."

"We have come very close the past two years to achieving the 'Best Places to Work" recognition in Georgia. Our employee turnover has kept us from being successful. That's why we are targeting that issue this year in our annual goals."
*

SGR Formula: $$\frac{(\text{Net Profit\%}) \times (1 + \text{Debt/Equity})}{(\text{Var. Assets\%}) - [\text{NPM\%} \times (1 + \text{Debt/Equity})]}$$

"Danny, 15 percent net profit seems very high for a business like yours," asked Faheer Zaruqi from across the room. "I wish we could net that much."
"It has to be that high Faheer," answered Danny. "I have too much money invested in this company and work too damn hard not to earn an

above-average return. Industry average is about 10 percent. A small price increase this year combined with a more efficient use of our service folks I think will get us there."

"What's up with the onboarding process?" shouted Theresa Mulsey from her seat across the room. "I read Bud's article last month titled *'Are You On-boarding or Waterboarding Your New Employees?'* Is that what you're doing? Torturing your new hires?

"Sometimes I think so," responded Danny. "We don't always make the new hires feel as welcome as we would like, I think. Last month a guy showed up for his first day and we had completely forgotten he was coming in. Not a good start. Now we use a new hire checklist that covers what happens the week before their first day, the first day, the first week, and the first month. Very detailed. It's made a huge difference."

"Danny, would you mind sharing that checklist with the group?" inquired Tex Alexander.

"It'll cost you my good friend," Danny responded with a wide grin. "I can't just be giving all this good stuff away."

"Take it out of your 15 percent profit Danny. I need that checklist. We really suck at bringing new people on. It's like a revolving door at our place."

"Okay, consider it a gift Tex. Might cost you a golf game."

"There are three components of that onboarding checklist that we have found to be very important." Danny shared with the group.

"The first item is that there has to be continuous communication between the new employee and our team between the time the individual has accepted the job and when they start. I remember a year ago hearing that Vistage speaker talk about companies like ours getting 'ghosted' by new hires. Never showing up for the first day. I think the percentage was close to 25% never making it to work the first day. Amazing! We have found that by amping up the communication pre-start, they are far more likely to show up on their first day."

"Next, we have found it is imperative that the new employee have a significant conversation with their immediate manager within the first seven days of their start date. The purpose of that meeting is to make sure the new hire is on track that first week and has everything they need to be successful. Also, in case there is an issue that first week it gets handled quickly."

"Last, we host a luncheon for that new employee at the end of the first week. A celebration. I could never figure out why companies will have a party for when an employee leaves but not when they start. That seems backwards to me. We like to celebrate their beginning and not their end."

"Danny, talk about the new COO. That's a new one for us. Are you getting lazy on us?" asked Dominique Patrick sitting right next to Danny.

"It's time," responded Danny emphatically. "I currently have fifteen direct reports including all of my area managers. That's too many. Way too many meetings. A good COO would reduce my number to five or six directs. That's more manageable and will allow me to work more on the strategic growth initiatives I have outlined for this year."

"I read Gino Wickman's book, 'Rocket Fuel', last year. He talks about the need for both a 'Visionary' and a 'Integrator' for a company to sustain growth. I am the visionary and definitely not the integrator. I need some-one to keep the train on the tracks on a daily basis. That's the job of the COO."

"Where will you find this COO?" Bud Irvine asked Danny.

"I have one internal candidate and one external candidate at this moment. The third option would be to acquire a smaller competitor with a solid operations person. This will be an expensive hire so I need to be right on this one."

The group continued with several more inquiries about Danny's business plan. He was well versed in it and appreciated the group's interest. He scrib-bled several notes as the questions continued.

CHAPTER 11
THE HOST PRESENTATION...
THE FINANCIALS

*"Revenue is vanity, profit is sanity,
and cash flow is reality."*
– Unknown

The next section of Danny's host presentation was his financials. Rather than share his financial statements with the group, Danny opted to share his financial dashboard. He had adopted this from a previous Vistage speaker several years earlier. The dashboard used trailing twelve-month charts tracking four Key Performance Indicators (KPIs): revenue, gross margin, operating expense as a percent of revenue, and net profit.

The trailing twelve-month charts (TTM) are particularly useful. Rather than depicting monthly numbers over a three-year period, each data point on the TTM represents 12 months of data. This eliminates any seasonal distortions to the data on the graph. Better data means better decisions for the user.

A recent Vistage speaker described this type of financial dashboard as being similar to the dashboard in your car. The auto dashboard indicates the operational health of the car, including the amount of gas left, engine temperature, oil pressure and so on. If there is a problem with the car, it will more than likely show up on the dashboard.

The financial dashboard for a business is the same way. It demonstrates to the business operator the financial health of the company using simple-to-read charts. If the business is healthy, the charts are usually trending upward. If there is a performance issue, the chart will indicate that to the business operator. Then, the operator can take a deeper dive into the financial statements to find out where the problem lies.

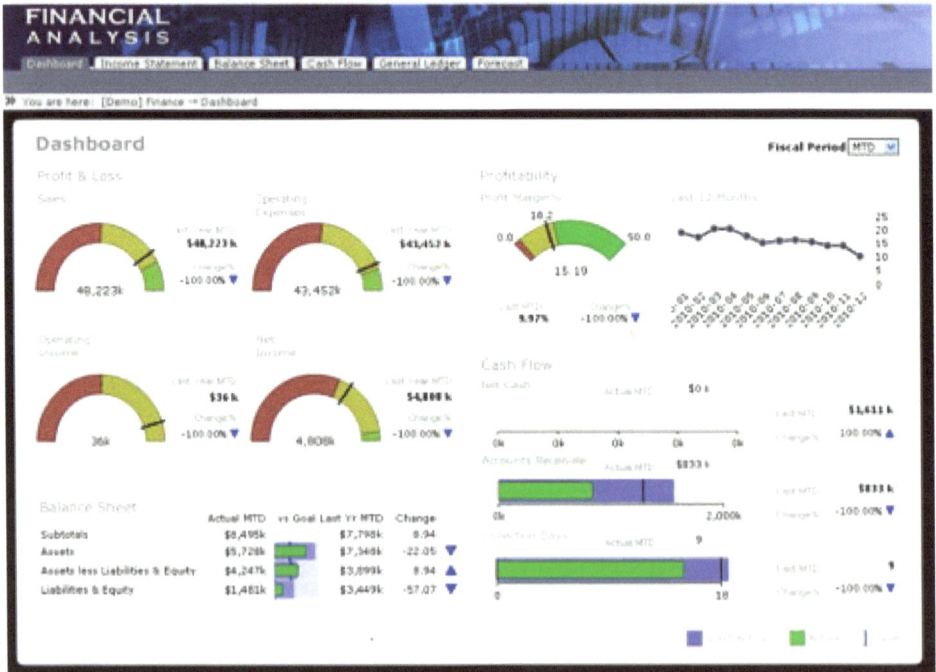

"Danny, your revenue chart looks mostly flat the past 18 months and yet your profits have trended upwards. How did this happen?" asked CPA Trace Webster.

"Good catch Trace," responded Danny with a grin on his face. "Two things happened there. One, we raised our prices last year 3 percent across the board. That incremental cash fell beautifully right to the bottom line for us."

"Secondly, we moved to a subscription revenue model last year. Rather than bill customers after a visit, we now bill them on the first day of the month whether we visit or not. Far more efficient and predictable revenue stream now. And it has added several additional points of net profit."

"That's genius, Danny", yelled Tex Alexander from across the table. "I wish we could get our customers to subscribe to us building their houses. We don't get paid until the punch list is completed and our crews have disappeared, and even then we don't always get all of our money. Cash is always tight."

"The other big number for us to watch is our Z Score," said Danny. "I learned this when I took that GrowSmart class at the Small Business Development Center at UGA. It's like a credit score for a business. Similar to what the bankers use to make credit decisions."

"The Z Score was invented by a professor to predict if and when companies are heading for bankruptcy. It takes into consideration four different financial measurements: liquidity, long-term profitability, short-term profitability, and leverage (debt/equity). If your number is below 1.6, you are in trouble. Somewhere between 1.6 and 2.5, you are at risk and above 2.5 you're okay."

"What's your Z Score Mr Goodall?" asked his friend Tony Barnett.

" 7.5 and rising sir," he responded quickly. "We like to see that number go up every quarter."

Danny spent the next five minutes answering several more questions on his financials and then moved to the org chart. Rather than show a traditional organizational chart, members instead shared a Three-Year organizational chart with the group. The three-year chart assumed a certain rate of growth over the next three years and then illustrated what the org chart will be for that company three years from now.

Danny's three-year chart showed several new positions to be added with growth and several new offices to open. He told the group that he liked to share this chart with both his existing employees as well as job applicants for them to see future employment growth opportunities within the company. He called it his "people" plan. He found it in Michael Gerber's best-selling book "*The E Myth*".

Next, Danny described his exit strategy to the group.

"I'll keep it simple my friends," Danny started, "I am looking at no less than ten years before I exit. Let's take her public or bring in private equity to scale outside the southeast. Maybe even an ESOP. I'll need no less than $10 million and then I 'll spend the rest of my life playing golf. Any questions?"

The members all smiled because they knew Danny would exit sooner for the right number and his wife would never allow a lifetime of golf.

"Danny, you have two young kids. Why not allow them the life of leisure in pest control? posed Randy Sapatana. "A strategic buyer here sounds like a competitor in disguise and they won't pay you what you want."

"My kids are way too smart to get involved in this mess," Danny responded. "There's a reason I'm spending $50K a year on their private school education. Pest control isn't quite sexy enough for them at this point."

Danny grinned as he was reminded that he started off in law school before he went to work in the family business and eventually bought his father out of the business.

The last ten minutes of his host presentation was consumed with reviewing his annual personal goals with the group. More travel and a lower golf handicap topped his list of goals.

Danny wrapped up his host presentation at the top of the hour. He was both exhausted and relieved that he had finished his presentation. It was time for a 10-minute break and then a transition into the Executive Session.

CHAPTER 12
THE EXECUTIVE SESSION

"I am not a product of my circumstances.
I am a product of my decisions."
– Stephen Covey

Bud always looked forward to the Executive Session portion of the group meeting for several reasons. First, it was a great opportunity for individual members to get help from the group on their most pressing business or personal issues. Second, it was also a great opportunity to learn from their peer's experiences, both good and bad. Third, for Bud as the group Chair, it was the most interesting part of the day.

Member issues showed up in the group meeting in a number of ways. Sometimes, the issue would originate in the monthly one-to-one meeting

that the Chair had with the member. The CEO would share a particular issue that he was stuck on or a decision she was working through. The Chair
would process that discussion for a while before asking the member if they
would like to bring the issue to the next group meeting for the group to
work on.

Some members were very happy to bring their issues to the group while
others dreaded that same experience. For some CEOs it was a golden
opportunity to get a group of smart business executives to share their
perspectives and experiences with the member in question, but for other members it was a stressful event to expose their apparent weakness or
blind spot to a group of their peers.

Aside from the one-to-one meetings, sometimes members would contact
the Chair prior to the group meeting to ask for time in the next meeting to
process their issue. To meet this need, Bud had a one page issue template
he would send to the member to complete prior to the group meeting. The
document would summarize the upcoming issue. The Chair would then
send that summary to the members before the group meeting so that they
could become familiar with the issue prior to the group discussion. Bud
always found that the better prepared everyone was prior to the meeting,
the better the group discussion.
Lastly, sometimes an issue would surface during the course of the group
meeting. Most often this would happen during the check-in when a member would casually mention to the group that he was "at war" with an
employee, or running out of cash, or possibly leaving his wife. Bud would
make a mental note of that issue and then offer to provide the member
group time that day to process the issue. Members rarely said no.

When Bud irvine went to San Diego for new Vistage Chair training more
than 15 years ago, he learned several methods for processing member
issues. The most common method had four distinct steps:

Step 1: Have the member take several minutes to introduce the issue to the
group. Share the facts and figures. Discuss the origin of the issue and why
it is important today. Who is impacted by this decision? What is at risk? Finally, what are the three (or more) possible options for resolving this issue?

Step 2: Now the member takes questions from the group. In the first round, the questions are clarifying in nature as members are collect pertinent information about the decision, filling in the gaps in what the member has already shared with them. These are questions about the impact of the issue, such as who is involved in the issue or how long has it been going on.

Next, the group members begin to ask more strategic questions. These are tougher questions to formulate and tougher for the member to respond to. Often, the members are looking for blind spots. What is it that the member has not yet considered or might be oblivious to? Members are also seeking to determine if there is a more significant issue at hand that is not being addressed. This is very common in issue processing. For example, a single employee issue might turn into a much bigger discussion around a toxic corporate culture.

Step 3: The next portion of the issue processing is when the group members provide feedback, which can show up in several ways. It may be a perception of the issue at hand. It may be a recommendation based on their own prior experience. It may also be a prescription for moving forward. The member at hand is listening intently to the group's feedback and often taking notes.

Step 4: The final step in issue processing is when the Chair turns to the member and asks three questions:
"Was this discussion helpful?"
"What did you hear from the group?"
"What will you do next?"

The last question holds the member accountable for taking some action on this issue over the next thirty days before the next group meeting.

In more than 15 years as a Chair, Bud noted some of the biggest mistakes that members and groups make when processing issues. Here are several:

- **Too quick to solve the problem.** Most CEOs are good problem-solvers. They have to be. They spend much of their time giving answers and fixing problems. Bud found that in the Executive Session, some members wanted to practically skip asking any questions and go right to fixing the problem. This is a very dangerous approach in a group meeting and even worse in their own business setting.

- **Addressing the wrong issue.** In Bud's experience the issue that the group starts with is rarely the issue that the group winds up with. There is almost always a larger, more significant issue at the end. This requires great patience on the part of the group, the Chair, and the member to work towards the larger issue at hand.

- **Asking "why" questions.** The word "why" inherently makes people uncomfortable. It puts individuals on the defensive. It questions motives when there may not be a motive. While there may be particular instances to use "why" questions, Bud found that it was better to avoid them when possible.

- **Failure to properly define the issue.** Bud found that the best way to define the issue was in a question that started with "How to…" As an example, if the issue is a cash flow problem within a company, the issue might be stated as "How to fix the cash flow problem we now have?". By stating the problem this way, it ensures clarity for the group on the issue and also moves the discussion more towards a solution by not spending too much time on the cause and effects.

CHAPTER 13
"HE'S A TERRORIST"

"The best thing you can do for a good employee is to fire a bad one."
– Bob Thomson, Vistage Speaker

"Tex, you're batting lead-off today in the Executive Session. You made mention earlier in our check-in about having a terrorist on your management team. Tell us more about that," said Bud.

Tex's facial expression quickly changed from a broad smile on his face to a look of disgust. He had brought this same issue to the group once before several years ago and had hoped that he wouldn't have to bring it back again. It was a sore subject for Tex and one that had gotten progressively worse over the past year.

"You all remember my CFO David. He was originally hired by my dad many years ago before I graduated from Tech and joined the company. He didn't have CFO credentials at the time and certainly is not showing them now. The faster we grow, the less engaged he is in the company. He seems to be taking time off at the least opportune times like the end of the month closing. His financial reports are late and full of mistakes. And frankly, I just don't think he gives a sh**!"

Bud interrupted Tex for a moment. "I think before we go any further, this is a good time to review the Welch Grid as Tex has referenced the 'terrorist' on his team."

The Welch Grid is believed to have originated with CEO Jack Welch at General Electric in 1991. Welch and his leadership team were looking for a more effective way of evaluating their talent. They decided that the two most important factors to consider were the employee's effectiveness (job performance) and their alignment to company values (employee behavior).

Bud Irvine approached the flip chart in the front of the room, grabbed a marker, and drew a big square with four quadrants inside of it. He labeled the horizontal axis of the square "job performance" and the vertical axis "behavior".

PERFORMANCE

	LOW	*HIGH*
HIGH	High Values Alignment *Cheerleaders* Low Performance	High Values Alignment *Super Stars (15%)* High Performance
LOW	Low Values Alignment *Deadwood* Low Performance	Low Values Alignment *Terrorist* High Performance

COMPANY VALUES

"Tony, upper right hand quadrant. Above average job performance and above average behavior. What do we call this person?" asked Bud.

"That's me Bud." responded Tony Barnett with a big grin. "That's a super-star."

"I agree with both statements," said Bud.

"We may have to take that up as a separate issue," called out Will Kross with a sly look on his face. "More of a part-time superstar given his vacation schedule lately."

"Okay Will, how about the bottom right hand quadrant. Above average performance and below average behavior" asked Bud.

"That's a terrorist, Bud," said Will quickly. "Not me by the way".

"Right answer, sir, on both counts" replied Bud. "Lacey, you're next. Upper left hand quadrant. We have below average job performance and above average behavior. What is our term for these team members?"

"I know this one because I have more than my share of them. These are 'cheerleaders,'" recalled Lacey. "Fun people with great attitudes. But they are not getting the job done."

"Dave, last quadrant. Bottom left. Below average performance and bad behavior. What do we have here?"

"Bud, I am proud to say that I have rid myself entirely of these guys. This is 'deadwood'. Our last group discussion on this convinced me to fire the last two," responded Dave Borden. "And the interesting part? They both landed in much better jobs after I cut them loose. It was a win-win."

"Everybody clear on the Welch Grid before we move forward with Tex's issue?" Bud asked of the group.

Phil Balmer's hand jumped up. "Bud, please remind me how we arrive at these designations? Is it just a gut feeling?"

"Phil, in many cases it is just a gut feeling as we evaluate an employee's job performance and on the job behavior. However, we are far better off having good metrics to drive these determinations. Performance metrics along the horizontal axis and engagement and behavioral metrics on vertical axis. My experience is that most companies have the performance metrics and do not have the behavioral numbers."

The group took the next ten minutes to ask Tex clarifying questions. They included inquiries about the CFO's job responsibilities, his relationships with his peers, his job status, and compensation package.

"Tex, where would you put your CFO on the Welch Grid?"asked Cliff Junningham.

"Well, for sure lately he has not been doing his job. Our financial reports have been late and filled with mistakes. He blames others, but the responsibility is his to provide me with timely and accurate financials."

"How about a number from 1-10 on job performance, Tex?" asked Cliff.

"It's a four at best. He's good working with our investors. He's a schmoozer there. The banks run hot and cold on him. I had one banker last month tell me he thought David was 'full of sh**'. He tried to renegotiate a loan package with mostly fictitious numbers. The banker was pissed."

Cliff spoke up again. "How about a number on his behavior? Is he aligned with the company's core values? Does he play nicely with everyone?"

Tex responded practically before Cliff could finish his last sentence. "That's a two at best. I have people coming to me every day complaining about his attitude and rudeness. He's aloof. Too good for the rest of us. Never a kind word for anyone. A real SOB."

Trace Webster perked up from the other side of the room and spoke up. "Tex, I heard you call this guy a 'terrorist', but based on what you've shared with us he sounds more like 'deadwood'. Bottom left quadrant. Why is he still there?"

"Well, until you all got me thinking about this I did think of him as a terrorist. But you're right, he's 'deadwood' in the Welch Grid. He's been with us so long and he has the title of CFO, it's just hard to think of him as 'deadwood'", Tex explained to the group.

Bud jumped into the conversation to help move it forward. "Tex, now that we have established his position in the Welch Grid, what do you see as your options moving forward?"

"Bud, I remember the speaker we had last year on this Welch Grid, and he identified four possible options. The first and most popular option is to do nothing. I can't afford to do that. I've been putting up with this too long as it is."

Tex continued. "The second option, if I remember correctly, is to isolate the 'terrorist'. Move him out. I am not sure I can isolate David any more than he has already done on his own. He is already on an island so to speak. He has flexible work hours. He comes into the office sparingly. If I isolate him any further, it will only continue to impact his job performance."

"The third option is coaching. I'm done talking to him. My dad speaks to him on occasion but I know he's not willing to coach or mentor him. A friend of mine suggested maybe an executive coach for him, but I'm not sure that would work, nor do I want to spend that type of money on him. I also know that coaching for a 'terrorist' rarely works. He's not going to change his behavior with or without a coach."

'What's your fourth option Tex?" asked Bud.

"Cut him loose. Fire him," responded Tex loudly.

"What's preventing you from doing that?"asked Dominique sitting next to Tex. "Has he got pictures of you in a compromising way?"

Tex smiled at the thought of David holding him hostage in some way.

"Remember the speaker we had earlier this year that talked about the 'J Curves'?" Tex asked the group.

"I am looking at one big 'J Curve' if I fire David. He knows where all the skeletons are hidden. He developed all of our financial systems. He has key relationships with our investors, bankers, and many vendors. It would take us ninety or more days and probably cost us low six figures to fire David."

"What are you fearful of Tex?" asked Theresa Mulsey in a soft voice.

"Three things. I am fearful of what this will cost the company. We're running on very tight margins right now as it is. I am also fearful that I will not be able to find another CFO for this job. Lastly, I am fearful that I'm wrong. Maybe he's not the problem."

The room got very quiet.

Breaking the uncomfortable silence, Bud posed one of his favorite questions. "Tex, if you brought in a hired gun to run the company. Top-notch, a no 'bs' executive. What would that person do in this situation?"

"I hate that question Bud," complained Tex. "He would fire him right away. It's a no-brainer."

"Tex, if your CFO came marching into your office this afternoon and tendered his resignation, would you accept it?" asked Theresa Mulsey sitting right across from her friend.

"In a heartbeat, Teresa. That's a no-brainer." responded Tex.

Dominick Patrick raised her hand next. "Knowing what you know about your CFO, if he left for a year and came back; would you rehire him?"

"Not a chance, Dominick. He has burned way too many bridges."

Tex then paused for what seemed like an eternity but was actually about fifteen seconds. His eyes took one slow lap around the room and then he stood up.

"That's it. I will terminate David before the end of the week. I owe it to my investors and more importantly to my people. Keeping a 'terrorist' makes me a 'terrorist' and that's not my calling. He's gone."

Once again, the room got very quiet before one by one each member stood and applauded.

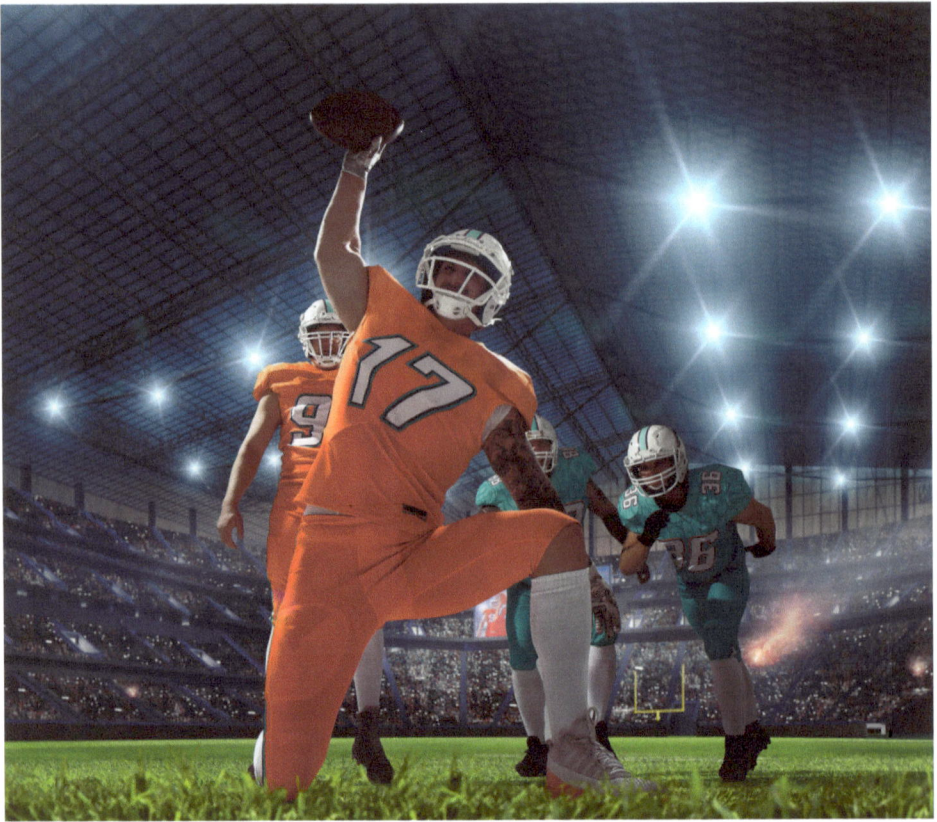

CHAPTER 14
"HOW DO I GET OUT?"

"I've accomplished a lot in my life, but what happened in the end zone is what defines my career."

– Elmo Wright, professional football player

"Ray, you're next," announced Bud after a brief meeting break. "You were our meeting host last month and I believe you owe us an exit strategy."

Ray Jernath had hosted the previous meeting and when it came to sharing his exit strategy in his host presentation there was a very uncomfortable silence. The group pressed him hard on it and Ray promised to work on it and share it at the next group meeting.

There was no other topic in the world that made Ray more stressed to think about or address than this one. Ray was President of a third-generation food processing company located just east of downtown Atlanta by Grant Park. With about $15 million in annual revenue, it was a healthy company with good margins.

Ray's parents were still alive but not actively involved in the business. He was single with two middle-aged sisters, both of whom had their own professional careers. His cousin, Jerry, was his operations manager. Jerry had no ownership interest and was planning to retire soon.

The exit strategy template the group used came from Atlanta author Patrick Ungashick and his book "Dance in the End Zone." The book identifies seven questions that the business owner must address in developing an exit strategy.

"Dance in the End Zone"
Seven Questions

1. When do you want to exit?
2. What is your most likely exit strategy?
3. How much is your Magic Number?
4. Where will it come from?
5. What risks do you face prior to exit?
6. What will you do after exit?
7. Who is on your exit planning team?

"Ray, the first question is about timing. When do you want to exit?" asked Bud Irvine.

"Ten years," responded Ray.

"Oh boy, here we go again," snorted Phil Balmer with a frown on his face.

Phil Balmer was recalling when Ungashick spoke to the group and shared that ten years was the most popular stated timeframe for an exit strategy and that it was typically code for "I don't know".

"Phil's right," Bud said to Ray. "Ten years doesn't work. We need a range of time. A 'not before' and a 'not after.'"

"Okay," Ray responded. "Let's say not before five years because that's when the new Beltline real estate development is projected to come by our facility and not after seven years because I will then be 65 years old and ready to move on."

"Beautiful Ray, it's taken us ten years to get that bit of information from you" yelled Theresa Mulsey with a big smile on her face.

Bud continued with his questions. "Ray, the next question is what is your most likely exit strategy?"

In his book, Ungashick describes four possible exit strategies. The first is a "Passer". The passer plans to transition the business to a family member. This could be a spouse, a son or daughter, or even an extended member of the family.

The second option is an "Innie". This option entails passing or selling the business to one or more employees of the business. It could be a key executive, a management team, or the entire employee population (ESOP).

The third option is an "Outie". This means selling the business to an outside buyer. Examples might include a competitor, a financial buyer like a private equity group, or possibly a strategic buyer. Most research indicates that a strategic buyer pays the highest multiple for a business.

The fourth and final option for exiting the business is a "Squeezer". The squeezer will just shut the business down upon exit. No sale. No real value to the business at closure. Many small service providers find themselves being "squeezers" when they exit. They just stop doing business.

"Ray, I know you're not a squeezer," Trace Webster declared. "Way too much value in that real estate, your customer base, and your brand to do that."

"That's correct Trace," responded Ray. "I also have no family members or employees that are either interested in the business or capable of buying the business. No question I am looking at an "Outie" exit strategy at this time.

"Third question Ray is your "Magic Number". How much money do you need to walk away with at the time of exit?' asked Bud.

"Well fortunately I have been saving for a number of years. I think the business is worth between $5 and $10 million now. So let's say my Magic Number right now is $10 million."

"Ray, is that enough?" asked Tony Barnett. "You are accustomed to a very comfortable lifestyle. Lots of travel."

"$10 million is plenty for me," responded Ray. "I have no heirs. I have invested well. No debt. Should be more than enough."

"That's great Ray" yelled Lacey Sutton with a big smile on her face. "I have two starving kids and a second mortgage on the beach house that's screaming for a sugar daddy. Let's talk after the meeting."

"Ray, I want to come back to that valuation for a moment." asked Danny Goodall. I remember reading in Ungashick's book that there were several significant factors that might cause the value of the business enterprise to go up or down. Do you mind if we explore those for a second?"

"Go ahead Danny. Rain on my party." Ray responded with a smile.

"First, customer diversity is important. Do any of your customers command more than 15 percent of your total revenue?"

"That's not any easy question." responded Ray. "Lots of different restaurants around town sell our beef, but we actually sell directly to national distributors that then sell to those restaurants. Easy answer to your question is yes. More than 50 percent of our sales go through one distributor and I know that is risky for a potential buyer of my company."

"It is," responded Danny. "Another question, if I may. How important are you to the success or failure of the business? If you disappear for some reason, can the business continue to thrive?"

Ray now got a very serious look on his face. "I'm afraid not. I manage all of the relationships with the vendors, the end users, the bank, and the feds. If I go, the business will likely go with me."

"Last question Ray." Danny stated. "How fast do you get paid?"

"That one I feel good about." responded Ray. "We get paid by the 10th day for every invoice and we pay our supplier every 30 days. Cash flow is good."

"I like that answer." Danny replied. "I think the first two need your immediate attention if you're going to get your $10 million selling price."

Bud now resumes his questions. "Ray, we're now on the fourth question. That $10 million. How much will you have saved up versus how much will you need to get when the sale of the business closes?" asked Bud.

"I think it's about 50-50. Again I have saved well the past ten years. I actually think the business is worth more than $5 million with the real estate, so I may see more than $10 million when I'm done.

"Fifth question, Ray. What risks do you face prior to exit?"

"Bud, I see three big risks and I lie awake at night worrying about them all frequently."
"The first risk is an external threat. How much longer will we be eating burgers? That's our main product and I am now seeing more and more of these 'fake' burgers with no meat. Some of our own restaurant customers are now adding these to their menus. SOBs!"

Ray's company was one of the leading providers of hamburger patties in the state.

"The second risk I face is if something happens to either Jerry or myself. We run a lean management team. In fact, we are the management team. If something happens to either one of us there might be a much quicker exit than I had planned on. Not a good situation."

"The third and final risk is the neighborhood we are in. It has changed dramatically in the past five years. Gone mostly multi-family residential. I am not sure how we fit into that change or what effect it might have on our exit. I may just be better off selling the land for residential development and relocating the business."

Bud continued. "Ray, the sixth question is my favorite. What will you do after exit?"

"Bud, what was that statistic that you shared with us a year ago about the lifespan of a CEO post-exit?" asked Dave Borden.

"Dave, it was seventeen months." responded Bud.

The room got very quiet all of a sudden as that number began to sink in for each of the CEOs gathered at the table.

"That can't be accurate," shouted Faheer Zaruqi standing up behind Ray Jernath. "Why so short?"

Bud Irvine was used to getting such an emotional response every time he shared this statistic. The reasoning for it is fairly intuitive. First, the act of exiting the business can be a very stressful event for a CEO. The leader is used to working long hard hours doing important work and then they exit and transition to a much easier and slower lifestyle. The brain is now working at a much different level than it was accustomed to and begins to die very slowly. The body goes next.

"I plan to be very busy when I exit," interrupted Ray in the group discussion.

"I am currently on several nonprofit boards and I expect to amp that up upon retirement. I also want to travel the world, starting with Europe. Lastly, I have several nieces and nephews that I can't wait to spend more time with."

"He'll be lucky to get to seventeen months," said Trace Webster. "That sounds more like torture than retirement Ray. I say the over/under is fifteen months. Anyone in on this bet?"

All of a sudden Ray's facial expression changed for the worse as he saw several of his colleagues take the "under" on his post-exit life expectancy.

"We better move to the final question Ray," said Bud. "I feel a sense of despair as you consider your early retirement."

"Last question. Who is on your exit planning team?"

"That's an easy one Bud. My CPA, our corporate attorney, my financial advisor, and my immediate family members. We actually had a meeting earlier this year to begin to answer some of these questions you've asked me today. We decided to meet twice a year moving forward. I also see this group as a part of that exit planning team as well."

"Nicely done Ray. That's a good start.

The group all stood and applauded Ray as he finished his interrogation.

CHAPTER 15
"IT'S TIME FOR A DIVORCE!"

"Divorce isn't such a tragedy. A tragedy's staying in an unhappy marriage. Nobody ever died of divorce."
– Jennifer Weiner, Fly Away Home

"Phil, I believe you're next. Is this a business partner issue?" asked Bud.

"I'm afraid it is, Bud. The situation has gotten very bad with my business partner. I need to start looking at a buy-out I'm afraid," responded Phil Balmer with a look of disgust on his face.

Phil Balmer and his partner Tom Gleason started Peachtree Office Furniture almost twenty years ago. Both men were just out of college and both had limited experience selling office furniture in Metro Atlanta. Neither were short on ambition at the time and a business partnership was in the making. With less than ten thousand dollars in combined savings, the two men negotiated a distribution deal with one of the largest office furniture manufacturers in the United States and started selling from their respective trucks.

Within three years, Peachtree Office Furniture had an office in Roswell GA, eight employees including the two partners, and $5 million in annual sales. The business was profitable and producing positive cash flow. Both partners worked hard, played hard, and were in the midst of starting families. Like many business partnerships, there was no partnership agreement, no partner role descriptions, and no exit strategy.

In 2018, the picture of this business looked very different. Now the company had twenty-eight employees, averaged about $20 million in annual sales, was marginally profitable, and starving for cash. Sales had continued to grow while margins had shrunk. A lack of organizational design had resulted in high employee turnover, issues with client deliveries and installations, and poor cash flow management.

To add to Bill's problems, his partner Tom had recently gone AWOL. Missing in action. A litany of personal problems from a bad marriage to some severe health issues had sidelined Tom from the business for most of the past year. He was, however, still taking full paychecks from the business and partner distributions.

"Phil, let's start with defining the issue at hand. Please start with 'How to …'"

Phil looked puzzled for a brief moment and responded. "How to leave my business partner without doing undue harm to the stakeholders of the business and my financial stake in the business?"

Attorney Cliff Junningham jumped in immediately. "Phil, I see three separate issues in that question: split from your partner, protect your stakeholders, and do no harm to your investment. How about force ranking those for us in order of importance?"

"Protecting my employees, our vendors, and business partners goes first," Phil replied. "I have worked very hard to build those relationships. Some are very close friends outside of work. I'm not willing to destroy those."

Phil continued. "Next is splitting up from Tom. He's toxic now. I've had several employees leave the company recently because of his antics. He's no longer selling anything and he insists on taking more cash out of the business to pay his divorce attorney."

"I've worked hard to build my net worth but I am confident that if there is damage there I can repair it. My wife is completely on board with me on this one, thankfully."

"Phil, what do you see as your options at this point?" asked Theresa Mulsey sitting directly across from Phil.

Members were trained to always have at least three options for any issue they processed with the group and Phil was prepared for this question.

"Option one is to force a split with Tom and I take over 100% ownership of the company. Option two is to walk away from the business. Let Tom take it all. I would try to work out a payout and then go start my own firm. That's the nuclear option for me."

Dominique Patrick raised her hand very quickly. "Phil, would you actually do that? Nuclear may be too gentle a word for that option."

"I would Dominique, and yes, the fallout from that option would be huge."

"What's the third option, Phil?" asked Trace Webster standing up from across the room.

"The third option is the 'do nothing' option. My least favorite. Hope things get better. Sit tight another year."

"That's your worst option and probably the most common of the three," Trace replied. "I see a lot of very unhealthy business partnerships with all the companies I work with. Many of them just keep working together, tolerating each other until they are forced to act, and that's usually too late."

"Phil, which option are you leaning towards today?" asked Bud Irvine, working to keep the discussion moving forward.

"While option two has some appeal to it and option three is the easiest thing to do at this point, I am planning to move forward with option one. I am going to force him out, pay him a fair market price for his ownership, and part ways. It's time." Phil looked convinced that he was heading in the right direction.

Tex Alexander raised his hand with a question. "Phil, how will your partner respond to this option number one? Will he be surprised?"

"I think he wants out, Tex. He just needs the money. He won't be surprised by this."

Tex continued his questioning. "And your primary supplier, how will they feel about this change in ownership?

"I think they will be onboard with this decision. They've seen it coming. They may even be willing to help finance it," responded Phil.

Will Kross raised his hand for Bud to see. "Phil, I am glad you mentioned financing. How will you find the cash to buy out your partner?"

"That's a tough one, Will." You just sold one of your apartment complexes. How would you like to get into the office furniture business?"

"Not a chance my friend. Hard enough to make money in multi-family housing. I'll stick to what I know." Will said with a smile. "But I am interested in knowing how you'll finance this deal."

Phil was quick to come back. "I have recently talked to my banker. Assuming a valuation of my business of $2 million, that's based on four times annual net earnings, I will need a bank loan for roughly seventy-five percent of that and my partner will need to take a note for the remainder."

"Phil, we are working on several similar deals and I think your valuation might be low. I know that multiple is common in small businesses but your business has several factors going for it that might justify a higher valuation," added CPA Trace Webster.

"Thanks Trace. I may need your help with this one." responded Phil. "Last question Phil. How will your employees react to this change in leadership?" asked Tex.

"That's a good question, Tex." Phil replied. "I think some of the more tenured employees may miss him. The newer guys will be very happy. We have actually lost a few key employees this past year due to this issue. Too much angst and uncertainty between the two of us has caused a toxic culture at times in the office."

"Phil, as the lone attorney in this group," Cliff said, "it is my obligation to tell you that this could get very messy. Partnership splits are rarely easy to settle and my sense is that your partner is going to want more than his fair share. Please let me know if I can help you get this started." Cliff had negotiated more than his share of partnership dissolvement cases and knew that Phil was in for a battle.

Bud could sense that the group members were starting to lose some steam as the clock passed 2:30 p.m.

"Phil, nice work presenting this issue to the group. We will expect a follow-up next month. Group, let's take a short break and come back for the final issue of the day."

CHAPTER 16
"WE'RE STUCK!"

"When everything seems to be going against you, remember that the airplane takes off against the wind, not with it."
– Henry Ford

Members slowly returned to the conference room. They always looked forward to the afternoon break because a group tradition decreed there would be a plate of warm chocolate chip cookies in the break room. Rarely were there ever any leftovers.

Bud stood and got the group's attention. "Okay, let's take out seats ladies and gentlemen. Last issue discussion of the day and we may have saved the best for last. Dave Borden, please tell the group what's going on."

Dave had been relatively quiet during the meeting, which was unusual. As one of the original members of the group, Dave enjoyed these meetings and typically was an active participant. Today was different.

"Bud, I've been stewing about this issue all day. Not sure it's worth the time of the group. Very frustrating to me." shared Dave with the group.

Randy Sapatana immediately spoke out. "Dave, if it's bothering you then it's worth our time. What's the issue?"

Dave Borden had been the CEO at Glow Paint, the U.S. division of a large German conglomerate, now for almost ten years. There had been steady growth over that time from $40 million in annual revenue to over $100 million. The 2008-10 recession slowed their growth, particularly in the commercial markets but the company rebounded in 2011.

"I think we're stuck," said Dave to the group. Revenue has been flat the last twelve months and I don't know what to do."
Dave passed out a chart showing revenue that past three years and it actually looked like a decline in sales the past six months.

"Dave, how do you explain the slump in sales?" asked Ted Alexander. "You and I both know the housing market is relatively strong."

"We're not much into the residential market, Ted, aside from large multi-family buildings. It's our commercial work that seems to be lagging now." responded Dave.

"How are your margins, Dave?" asked Danny Goodall.

"Danny, our gross margins have dipped slightly year to date. Production costs have inched up and the Germans keep adding their own expenses to our costs. Our operating margins have stayed pretty consistent thanks to some efficiencies in the production facilities."

Tony Barnett raised his hand and got the attention of Chairman Bud. "Dave, what type of growth had you planned for this year?"
"Good question, Tony", responded Dave. "We actually were planning on an 8 percent growth on the top line this year. We thought that between the

growth in the economy and several new sales initiatives, this was a relatively safe growth goal. Looks like we have misfired so far."

Randy Sapatana spoke next. "Hey Bud, we had that Vistage speaker earlier in the year that talked about growth and he identified four ways to grow. I remember acquisition was one of them. What were the other three?"

"Good memory Randy", replied Bud. "I still have that list in my notes." Bud then proceeded to write the following list on the flip chart.

Four Ways to Grow
#1. Fix (better, faster, cheaper)
#2. Innovation
#3. Scaling (building capacity)
#4. Acquisition

"Dave, discuss each of these options as they apply to your issue." asked Bud. "Well, I'll start with **"fix"**. We were having some shipping issues earlier in the year and I think we have addressed those problems. We had an under-performing sales rep in the Northwest region whom we have now replaced. Lastly, we were having some quality issues with one of our top-selling products and I think we have fixed that issue."

Dave continued. "I am pretty satisfied with our **innovative** efforts this year. We have introduced several new products to our offering that have been in R&D for some time. One product in particular has gotten some early traction with our commercial builders in the Northeast. We have also been able to automate some of our marketing efforts that has reduced time in the sales cycle and also allowed us to reduce headcount in the marketing department by two people.

"**Scaling** the business model has been a challenge for us this year. We have limited space to grow in our production facility. They are very cramped there now for more room. We could add another big mixer in there. I am also reluctant to add headcount with flat sales. I have considered adding two more outside sales reps. And we had some folks from Georgia Tech's economic development team visit our plant recently and they think we could further automate our manufacturing processes and possibly add 25-50 percent more production capacity."

Dave took a needed breath for a moment and looked at the last item on the flip chart.

"I have not ruled out an acquisition, but it won't happen this year. The German owners have ruled out any capex money for this year. It's unfortunate. There is a smaller competitor in Wisconsin that reached out to us. The owner wants to retire and sell the business. They have a product we don't have that would fill a void in our offering."

Will Kross raised his hand next. "Dave, what happens if you finish the year with no sales growth?"

Dave frowned as he heard the question. "The German owners are not happy. We are their largest market. They expect growth and more importantly the cash that comes with growth. I'm feeling more pressure today than I ever have from ownership to expand our market share."

"Hey Dave." Lacey Sutton was now waving her hand at her friend across the table. "We had that speaker last year talk about calculating our Sustainable Growth Rate. A safe growth rate for a business. Have you calculated yours lately?"

Bud remembered that speaker and his description of Sustainable Growth Rate. It was a function of profitability as measured by net profit, risk calculated by the debt to equity ratio, and scalability as measured by the variable asset percentage.

"12 percent Lacey", responded Dave. "I looked at that just last month. Our profitability is okay. We are under-leveraged on the balance sheet. Very little debt. And with all of the equipment in the plant our variable asset percentage was relatively low. All in all, we should be growing faster."

Ray Jernath rose to his feet next, stretched, and then spoke to Dave. "Last month we had that speaker say something that really stuck in my head. May I share it with you?"

Ray moved towards the flip chart and proceeded to write the following:
"Your business is operating exactly as it is designed to operate".

Ray continued. "Dave, this might sound crazy. Is it possible that your business today is designed to not grow revenue?"

Dave now had a flustered look on his face. "I have not thought about it that way Jay", Dave responded. I think we have just assumed that growth was inevitable after we had had consistent growth for so many years. Maybe that was a false assumption."

"I have a different possibility Dave," stated attorney Cliff Junningham. "Bud had us all read Jim Collins new book 'The Flywheel' earlier this year. I am wondering if you are currently experiencing the 'flywheel effect' in your business?"

"Cliff, I think I missed that meeting," responded Dave. "Please remind me what the Flywheel Effect is."

Bud Irvine remembered the Flywheel Effect clearly because he had encountered it with a number of his members the past year. Author Collins describes the Flywheel Effect emergeswhen companies are working very hard to achieve results and not seeing immediate or short-term progress on those results. Sometimes, he explains, it's a timing issue. The results just don't happen immediately or as soon as we would like. But if we keep pushing, exerting effort, it is possible that the results will occur and sometimes even with less effort than before.

"Cliff, I hope that's the case," said Dave. Maybe we need to be more patient and allow some of the changes we have made to gain some traction before we expect to see results. I guess in today's world we just expect everything to happen faster."

Bud Irvine decided it was time to redirect the group discussion. "Dave, what do you now see as your three best options for igniting the growth in sales that you and your German owners want?"

Dave took a moment to respond to Bud while the Chair moved towards the flip chart to record his response.

"First option is to amp up our sales and marketing efforts. My CMO (Chief

Marketing Officer) has been asking for more resources and I have been hesitant to make that commitment. He wants $100,000 for a national conference and a direct mail campaign. My Sales VP is waiting on me to approve two new hires for sales rep positions."

"Sounds like you may be the bottleneck in this whole deal, Dave." shouted Phil Balmer from the opposite side of the room.

"Very possible, Phil. I remember Bud telling us that the 'bottleneck in most organizations is almost always at the top of the bottle,'" responded Dave with a grin on his face.

"What's your second option, Dave?" asked Bud.

"Option two would be to make another run at that acquisition I mentioned earlier. That would give us a quick bump in top-line revenue as well as addressing some of the production issues we have experienced recently. I just need to get ownership to buy into that deal. They have the cash to make that happen."

"Last option is to do nothing. Not my favorite choice. Maybe I just need to be more patient with what we are already doing. Let the flywheel do its magic."

"Dave, which option are you leaning towards today?" asked Bud.

"I think it may be a hybrid approach. I can approve several of the hires today along with $75,000 for more marketing. I am also going to call my acquisition target on Monday and schedule a trip to go see him this month. I think he may still be interested in moving forward. Last, I want to call my senior management team together next week and review our annual plan and see what's already working and what needs to be adjusted. I need to see some evidence of that flywheel effect."

As Dave was speaking, Bud was taking a full page of notes on the flip chart for him.

"Very good Dave. The group will expect a 30 day report on this issue next month at our next meeting," stated Bud.

"Thanks guys. This was a very helpful session. I have a much clearer perspective on this issue now than I had an hour ago. I will have much to report next month." reported Dave with a grin on his face for the first time all day.

"Okay group, let's take a quick timeout and we will come back to wrap up the day' s meeting. I think I still see several chocolate chip cookies left on the table." Bud announced.

CHAPTER 17
MEETING ADJOURNED

"Great is the art of beginning,
but greater is the art of ending."
– Henry Wadsworth Longfellow

The group took their seats and prepared for the closing session of the day's meeting. They looked both tired and inspired by the day's events.

Bud was always amazed at how fast the meeting day passed. Parts of the day already seemed to be a blur in his mind.

Just as the day started off with a member check-in, Bud also felt it was equally important that the meeting finish with a final check-in. A rapid recall of sorts.

"OK, folks, let's begin to wrap things up today," announced Bud to the group. "Let's do a quick rapid recall. What are you taking away from today's meeting? What did you learn?"

Ray Jernath raised his hand first. "Great meeting today Bud. The time the group spent on my issue today was priceless. I need to zero in on my Exit Magic Number and put my exit strategy into writing."

Cliff Junningham was next. "I enjoyed seeing Danny's One-Page Business Plan this morning and I was reminded that I need to finish mine before I host next month. Putting all that stuff on one page is a great idea and it makes it easy to communicate what's important to our team members."

Sitting next to Cliff was Phil Balmer. "I have a much better perspective on my partner issue today thanks to the group discussion. Funny how what started out so well as a partnership could end up so badly today. I guess that's true with so many partnerships, both business and personal."

"Faheer, you're next." stated Bud working to keep the reporting moving forward.
"Bud, I really enjoyed the discussion we had this morning on Core Values when Danny did his host presentation. Very enlightening. We have core values, but I'm not sure they're being used like Danny's group does. We need to revisit ours and put them to work."

Theresa Mulsey was prepared to go next. "I also enjoyed Danny's host presentation. We're good about setting annual goals but have never gone beyond that. I like his three-year goals. Forces the team to think a little further out timewise. I want to work with my team on setting our three-year goals."

Dominique Patrick spoke right up. "Bud, I need help calculating our Sustainable Growth Rate. I think we tried several years ago and it didn't make sense at the time. I wonder if we are growing fast enough today. That would be a very helpful calculation for my executive team to see."

Trace Webster was savoring his last chocolate chip cookie of the day and was prepared to go next. "The discussion this morning of the Visionary and the Integrator got my attention. I need to read that book. What was the title again?"

"'Rocket Fuel' by Gino Wickman" responded Bud. "I'll be curious which role you see yourself in when you finish reading the book Trace."

"Let's keep moving. Tex, you're next. What was your best takeaway of the day?"

Tex stood up and responded. "I am the terrorist. I remember that speaker we had last year who said 'You are what you tolerate.' I have been tolerating a terrorist for way too long which now makes me the terrorist. That ship has sailed. I will have a new CFO before we meet again my friends." Tex now had a broad smile on his face and the group applauded his announcement.

"Danny, great job hosting our meeting. What did you learn today?" asked Bud.

"First of all, I learned to buy more cookies. This group inhaled those suckers this afternoon. More importantly, the Welch Grid we looked at today was very helpful. I think I have a Terrorist like Tex that I need to eliminate. I also have several Cheerleaders that need to be addressed."

"Danny, the good news is that your Cheerleaders can be fixed. They have the potential to become Superstars. Your Terrorist is a different story. He must be removed," Bud added.

Tony Barnett was next. "Bud, I was reminded today how difficult business partnerships can be. They start off with all good intentions and then they all seem to implode at some point in time. One partner wants to go one way and the other has a different plan. And then trying to break up a partnership? What a mess. I have a hard enough time just maintaining my marriage. No business partners for me."

Randy Sapatana looked at his friend and neighbor Tony and smiled. "Hearing Dave's issue about business growth was very interesting for me today because we've been there. We've gotten stuck several times in our growth. We called it 'No Man's Land' because we were stuck and not making any money. Terrible place to be. We actually had to get smaller before we could get bigger."

"I agree with Ray," said Will Kross. "Great meeting today. Missed not having Carter here today. I am intrigued by this notion of a 'Flywheel Effect' because I think we are experiencing some of that today. It seems like we are pushing really hard for growth and not seeing any results yet. Should we back off? Push harder? Be patient? I need to read that book by Jim Collins. Thanks Bud."

Lacey Sutton looked up from her notes and went next. "I liked looking at Danny's financial dashboard. Kind of reminds me of the dashboard in my car. Gives me just enough data to know the car's performance is okay. I particularly like the Trailing 12- Month Charts. We use the traditional charts and get fooled by seasonality all the time. The TTM charts don't lie. Up is good. Down is bad. I need to have my CFO work on a dashboard like his for us."

"Dave, you have the last word today," stated Bud to Dave Borden.

"Bud, not to be over-dramatic but this meeting might have saved my business or even more important my career. I just could not get my arms around this issue with growth and just talking about it here with the group was amazing. I can't wait to get my executive team together on Monday to begin to explore the growth strategies we discussed here today. Thanks guys!"

CHAPTER 18
EPILOGUE

"At last, the wheel comes full circle"
– Cassandra Clare, Clockwork Princess

5 a.m. Aug. 12, 2018

It's hard for Bud to believe that six months have passed since that meeting in February. The group has met each month since. They've had several great speakers including Dave Nelson speaking on the life of Steve Jobs, Hunter Lott discussing HR Best Practices, and Rick Houcek presented on Strategic Planning.

The group has added two new members and had one member, Will Kross, sell his business and leave the group. Anytime a new member joins the group, the group dynamics always change and no member is ever replaceable.

But that February meeting continues to linger in Bud's mind now six months later. It was one of those meetings and much has changed since.

The meeting host that day was Danny Goodall. Danny was considering the hire of a new Chief Operating Officer (COO) that day. He ended up promoting one of his direct reports for that position and so far it has worked out quite well for everyone involved. The company is on track to hit all of its annual Key Performance Indicators (KPIs).

That hire has allowed Danny to spend more time on the strategic initiatives of the company. There may be a key acquisition before the end of the year. More importantly, he is now able to spend more time with his wife and two teenage children, Also, his golf handicap has dropped four strokes in just six months.

Bud also remembers member Tex Alexander discussing his issue with his "terrorist" that day. Tex fired that executive the following week as he promised the group. He told the group the next month it was the toughest and best decision of his career.
He then proceeded to engage an interim (part-time) CFO to help him fix the mess his previous CFO had created and to help him find and transition a new full-time financial executive. That new CFO started work for Tex last month and was hitting on all cylinders within his first thirty days. Tex is receiving accurate and timely financials for the first time he can remember.

Bud also remembers Ray Jernath facing a tough interrogation from the group that day on his exit strategy. For two months the group saw little action from Ray on his exit strategy. Then at the May meeting he promptly announced that he was planning to sell the business to a larger competitor for a nice profit and then sell the property to a real estate developer to build condos facing downtown Atlanta.

Ray was looking forward to serving on several nonprofit boards, teaching yoga, and traveling extensively. He seemed very happy that day.

And Bud?

Bud decided to retire at the end of the year. It had been16 years. Almost 1,000 meetings. More than 4,000 one-to-one meetings. Several hundred members. It was time to move on.

In his last meeting as a group leader, Bud shared several of his favorite rules for Chairing with his members.

- "I am only as good as the ground I stand on."

- "Marketing is like shaving. Do it every day or you will look like a bum."

- "Members will never care as much about the group as I do."

- "Trust the group."

- "Fail fast...this is a laboratory."

- "Leaders must act first and eat last."

- "You are what you tolerate."

- All of our conversations in life are with ourselves, there just happens to be other people around."

- "Your group is operating exactly as it is designed to operate."

LOOK FOR TIM'S OTHER
BOOKS ON AMAZON NOW

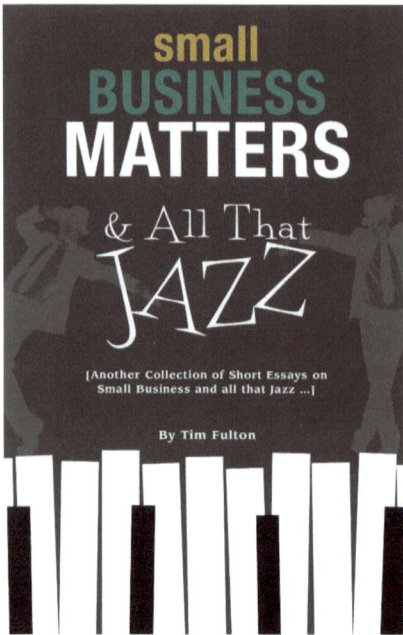

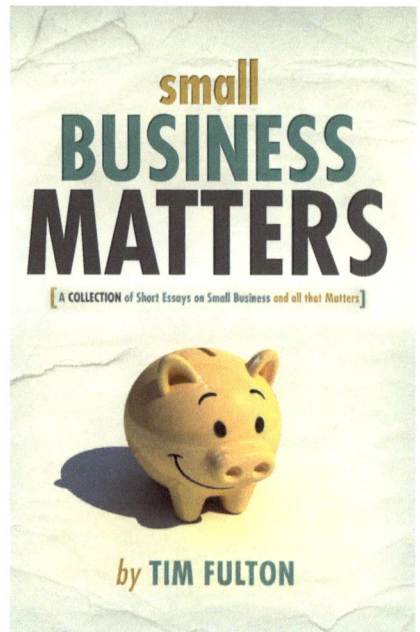

INTRODUCING THE
AUTHOR TIM FULTON

Tim grew up in Miami FL and attended college in New Orleans at Tulane
University where he earned an under-
graduate degree in Economics and a
5-year MBA.

He owned and operated several small
retail businesses in Miami. He also
taught as an adjunct professor and
served as the interim Director of the Family Business Institute at Florida
International University.

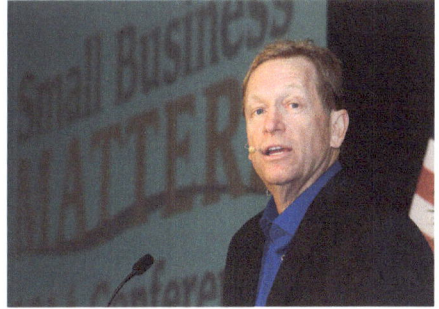

 After moving to Atlanta, Tim was a co-founder of an internet software
company that was an INC 500 company and then sold to a Fortune 1000
company. In 1992, he started his own small business consulting firm *Small
Business Matters.*

Tim was a Vistage Chair for 16 years, retired in December 2018. He currently enjoys Chair Emeritus status. In 2008, he developed the GrowSmart
training program for the state of Georgia and has trained over 2,000 small
business owners in 15 different states.

Tim has an award-winning *Small Business Matters* newsletter, has
self-published two books, and co-hosts a popular podcast. He also hosts
one of the largest annual events in Atlanta for small business owners.

He has been married to his college sweetheart Remy for 36 years, has two
grown sons, and is an avid tennis player. Tim has walked the entire 500-
mile El Camino Santiago in Spain on two different occasions in the past
five years.

ACKNOWLEDGEMENTS

This book would never have been possible without the unwavering support of many people starting with my wife Remy and two sons Taylor and Carter. My mom, Dorothy, was the best interrogator on the planet and taught me to ask great questions. My dad, Robert, taught me so much about business in a relatively short period of time.

I have a number of great friends who have supported this project in ways they could never comprehend. They know who they are and I thank them greatly.

Vistage International, the support team, and all of the amazing Chairs I have met the past twenty years have all contributed to the writing of this book. Specifically, I want to thank Bud Carter, Lisa Dugan, and Wade Bradley.

This book needed considerable editing and I am grateful to Cindy Miller, Edward Miller, and Kelly White for the time they each invested into taking my rough draft and making it readable.

Graphic artist Matthew Boyd is a master at making anything I do look 10x better. He is a creative genius.

Lastly, I want to thank my Vistage members who for 16 years shared their lives with me in ways they could never understand.